IF Y
WANT SO........ING
YOU NEVER HAD, THEN
DO SOMETHING
YOU NEVER DID
STORIES AND MAXIMS

By the same author

- Oriental Stories as Tools in Psychotherapy

- Positive Psychotherapy: Theory and Practice of a New Method

- Positive Family Therapy

- Psychotherapy of Every Day Life

IF YOU
WANT SOMETHING
YOU NEVER HAD, THEN
DO SOMETHING
YOU NEVER DID

STORIES AND MAXIMS

Nossrat Peseschkian

STERLING

STERLING PAPERBACKS
An imprint of
Sterling Publishers (P) Ltd.
A-59, Okhla Industrial Area, Phase-II,
New Delhi-110020.
Tel: 26387070, 26386209; Fax: 91-11-26383788
E-mail: mail@sterlingpublishers.com
www.sterlingpublishers.com

*If you want something you never had,
then do something you never did*
Stories and Maxims
Copyright © 2005, Nossrat Peseschkian
ISBN 978 81 207 6912 0
Reprint 2006, 2008. 2012, 2013

Printed in India

Printed and Published by Sterling Publishers Pvt. Ltd.,
New Delhi-110 020.

Foreword

In this interesting book titled *If you want something you never had, then do something you never did*, Prof. Nossarat Peseschkian brings out his rich experience and critical knowledge in conveying the message of Positive Psychotherapy which could help to address various interpersonal conflicts. He also successfully attempts to provide deep insight and a unique but simple technique, where the listener and reader can align his needs with a specific story. According to the author, the function of stories is to ignite the process of thinking about the common problems arising from day-to-day interpersonal relationships.

The appropriate use of stories is an intelligent method to invoke intuition and imagination as a useful resource to understand and resolve such problems that are commonly encountered in day-to-day situations.

The popularity of this book can be easily judged by the fact that since its original publication, the German edition has been reprinted more than a dozen times and it has become very popular with both professional and lay persons. Once you start reading it, you cannot stop till you finish it. This is the charm of this book.

The book has a universal appeal and I believe it will be equally popular with English readers.

Shridhar Sharma

MD, FRC Psy (Lond), DPM, FRANZCP (Australia), FAPA (USA) FAMS
Emeritus Professor
National Academy of Medical Sciences, New Delhi, India

Acknowledgement

The description of the cases have helped in better understanding of the theory and practise of (Are they translated into English.) psychotherapy. I would like to recommend my books *Positive Psychotherapy, Psychotherapy of the Day-to-Day Life, The Businessman and the Parrot and Psychosomatic and the Psychotherapy* to the readers who are interested in psychotherapy.

It would have not been possible to present this book in its present shape without the cooperation and openness of the patients and their willing approval to publish their case description. For the sake of originality, the verbal and written reports are being reproduced literally.

I would like to thank my secretaries Ms Monika Scheld and Ms Margot Duckgeischel for their consistence and patience. I would specially like to thank the Herder Publishing House. Above all I would like to thank all my colleagues, Dr Regina Rettenbach, Dipl. Psych-Hans Deidenbach, Dr Anas Azia, Dr Thomas Becker, Dipl. Psych. Adelheid Bieger, Dr Udo Boessmann, Dr Birgit Boenholf, Dr Claudia Christ, Dr Wolfgan Hoenmanna, Dipl. Psych. Abbass Jabbarian, Dipl. Psych. Dr Michael Katzensteiner, Dipl. Psych. Jutta Keller, Dr Marion Liermann, Dr Hamid Peseschkian, Dr Nawid Peseschkian, Manije Peseschkian, Dr Astrid Raile, Dr Arno Remmers, Dr Dorothee Teller, Dr Johannes Umlauf who have helped me through their experiences with patients, discussions and questioning to give a form to this book.

Contents

Sorrow or smile:
Life is too short for a long face

Scene 1:   *I am going down the street.*
                There is a deep hole in the way.
                I fall into it.
                I am lost...I have no hope.
                It's not my fault.
                It takes very long to come out.

Scene 2:   *I am going down the same street.*
                There is a deep hole in the way.
                I do as if did not see it.
                I again fall into it.
                I cannot believe I am again
                at the same place.
                But it is not my fault.
                It again takes very long to come out.

Scene 3:   *I am going down the same street.*
                There is a deep hole in the way.
                I see it.
                I again fall into it... out of habit.
                My eyes are open.
                I know where I am.
                It is my own fault.
                I come out of it immediately.

Scene 4: *I am going down the same street.*
There is a deep hole in the way.
I go round it.

Scene 5: *I am going down another street.*
"If you want something you never had, then do something you never did." This motto of positive psychotherapy is illustrated in this book with the story of The Wanderer, that runs like a thread through the entire book, and through case studies of people whose reactions to this story are worth telling.

My experience from many years of psychotherapeutic work can be summed up in a sentence. People feel over-exerted when confronted with abstract concepts and theories. Since psychotherapy is not a subject for experts alone, but serves as a bridge to patients–the non-experts, it needs to be easy to understand. Examples, stories, poems, maxims, and jokes, act as important tools in making the understanding easier. Although the fruit ripened in the European Occident, the roots of the tree bearing this fruit lie in the Persian orient, the country of my birth and youth. Thus, this book and I hope, my psychotherapeutic work represent an attempt to combine the knowledge of the Orient with the advances of the Occident problems. Nevertheless, I consider it useful, if not necessary, especially at a time when geographical distances are vanishing. The stories at the beginning of the chapters are, if not mentioned otherwise, created by me or are variations of stories from the rich oriental tradition.

**Own experiences are costly; others'
experiences are valuable.**

The following three principles of positive psychotherapy are at work in the stories and maxims:

- ◆ the principle of hope,
- ◆ the principle of balance,
- ◆ the principle of advice.

The concept of positive derives from the Latin *positum* that means the (actual), the 'pregiven'. Actual and pregiven are not only disturbances, illnesses, conflicts, and prejudices, but also the capability and possibility of resolving the conflicts, and the opportunity of understanding each other and working together, rather than against each other.

The aim of the story The Wanderer, which I narrated in my first book itself, was to elucidate the experiences and problems of patients, and to point to the fact that the "wanderer" - or the "sufferer" - needs help from others to become aware of his "blind spots", gradually get rid of his old habits and try new ways of life.

Then as "wanderer between two cultures", I recognised that each one of us is a "wanderer". Further, I recognised that the motive of the "wanderer" plays an important role in many cultures, philosophies, religions, and poems. The word "bewandert" (wandered, experienced) means: to know from one's own experience. "To wander" actually means to go here and there, to go somewhere, to change one's position.

One can stand on one's position but should not remain sitting on it.

Each topic in this book begins with a story and a maxim. Figurative thinking on the right half of the brain opens the door to fantasy.

To enable the shift from the general to the specific, I give case examples from psychotherapeutic, medical, family-therapeutic practice and from everyday life. First of all, some case examples in connection with the "wanderer" are described in short. These are followed by more detailed case examples, so that the reader finds it easy to develop strategies for overcoming his problems. The reader can interpret these stories himself and try to find what they have to tell him. He can exchange his ideas with his partner, his family or other people and perceive these discussions as a way of gaining experience.

The subsequent explanations address the left half of the brain. The purpose of these explanations is to work out the patient's background and motives to grasp the meaning of crises and opportunities, bright and dark sides, disturbances and capabilities.

"He who asks is your guide."

The hints given under "Broadening of goals", should serve to expand one's own views through new viewpoints, some from other cultures. Working up of problems, complaints and crises plays an important role:

◆ for mental and physical health,
◆ for the profession,
◆ for the family,
◆ for the future, including issues of world peace, understanding the meaning of life and life after death.

Last but not least, this book can be an oasis of relaxation through the humour contained in the many stories and maxims. It has been my experience that the stories have something adventurous and unpredictable in them. Trains of thought, desires and ideas, which we are familiar with and are accustomed to, appear suddenly in a new light; many things turn upside down.

It is never too early and never too late for learning; it is always the right time.

The Wanderer–
Why new ways of looking at things help

Persian mysticism tells of a wanderer who trudged along a seemingly endless road. He was loaded down with all sorts of burdens. Moaning and groaning, he moved forward step by step, complaining of his hard fate and the weariness that tormented him. On his way, a farmer met him in the glowing heat of midday. The farmer asked him, "Oh tired wanderer, why do you load yourself down with that boulder?" The wanderer replied, "Awfully foolish of me, but I hadn't noticed it before." With that, he threw away the rock, and felt much lighter. Again, after he had gone a long way farther down the road, a farmer met him and asked, "Tell me, tired wanderer, why do you trouble yourself with the half-rotten pumpkin on your head, and why do you drag those heavy iron weights behind you on chains?" The wanderer answered, "I'm very glad you pointed it out to me. I didn't realise what I was doing to myself." He took off the chains and smashed the pumpkin into the ditch alongside the road. Again, he felt lighter. But the farther he went, the more he began to suffer again. A farmer coming from his field watched him in amazement and said, "Oh good man, you are carrying sand in the sack, but what you see far off in the distance is more sand than you could ever carry. And your big water bar - this is as if you planned to cross the Kawir desert. All the while there's a clear stream flowing alongside you, which will accompany you on your way for a long time." The wanderer replied, "Thank you, farmer. Now I know what I have carried along." With these words, the wanderer tore open the water bar and emptied its brackish water onto the path. Then he filled a hole with the sand from his rucksack. He glanced down at himself, saw the heavy millstone around his neck, and suddenly realised it was the stone that was still causing him problem to walk so bent over. He unloosened it and threw it as far as he could, into the river. Freed from his burdens, he wandered on through the cool of the evening to find lodging.

A 51-year-old patient of depression read the story of The Wanderer. In the next sitting he was quite excited. He spluttered out a number of experiences and habits which he perceived as burdens. "I was always taught to be thrifty. And this habit has accompanied me till today. While trying to be thrifty I create such a mess that in the end this form of thriftiness proves to be costlier. For example, I go into the cellar to fetch something from my toolbox. But in order to be economical, I switch on only the staircase light and search in the half-lit cellar. When I don't find it, I turn the light on and find the object immediately. Thus the excessive thriftiness not only costs unnecessary time but also gets on my nerves. Even the maxim 'Be careful and think of safety!' has always been a burden for me. Fearing that something wrong could happen, I hesitate to start the work of repairing a cupboard, although I can do it very well. I keep postponing the work and feel quite burdened. After some time, when I do start the work, it goes very well. Subsequently, I have the feeling that my excessive need for safety and the fear of doing something wrong is almost the same as the rotten pumpkin on the head of the wanderer. But I have succeeded on my own to get rid of one or the other burden, and I am proud of it. When I wanted to construct a house my parents shuddered at the thought of financial burden. They repeatedly told me to be careful. But I had courage. With my hard work and with the help of my

15

wife, I succeeded in my efforts. The house is now built and the debts have been repaid except for a few mortgages. Inspite of this, I am still loaded with burdens hanging on me like rocks and chains. But I have recognised them to some extent and want to remove them, just like the wanderer did on his way."

The message of The Wanderer is clear. People laboriously drag themselves along the seemingly endless path of life, often not perceiving their own burdens. Other people one meets on this path can help in recognising the burdens, since they see them clearly. Till someone paints them out, one continues carrying all these burdens. Often the burdens go on adding up with the length of the path. Rocks get piled one on top of another and people do not notice how heavy their burden has become. They feel only fatigue and dullness. Moreover, people keep things which they think they may need. The wanderer was carrying sand and water although both these things were available near him in large quantities. Freed from the compulsion of carrying things that he could get anytime, the wanderer was also able to free himself from his biggest burden– the millstone. The millstone was making the wanderer over bend while walking. Thus he could not be an "upright person". The inability to honest will naturally reflect as a difficulty in dealing with oneself and other people.

In the case of the wanderer, it was only necessary to draw his attention to his burdens. He recognised them and got rid of them easily. It would be nice if people got on so well with one another that they could mutually, help each other.

Small things make up life–
The importance of ordinary matters

The right price

As King Anoschirwan was travelling through the land with his entourage, he came to a desolate area in the mountains where there weren't even any pathetic little shepherd huts. The King's cook lamented, "Noble Sultan! I am here to please your palate. But in our canteen we don't have even the tiniest grain of salt. And without salt the food tastes terrible. Noble Sultan, what should I do?" Anoschirwan replied, "Go back to the nearest town. There you'll find a merchant who has salt to sell. But be careful to pay the right price and not a bit more than is usual." The cook spoke, "Noble Sultan, in your chest you have more money than anyone else in the world. What difference would it make to you if I were to pay a bit more for salt? That little bit won't amount too much." The king looked at him gravely and answered, "It is precisely the little things that grow into the injustices of the world. Little things are like drops of water that eventually fill an entire lake. The great injustices of the world began as little things. So go and buy the salt at the usual price." (Persian story)

A 45-year-old engineer having psychosomatic complaints reports:

"What does the story The Wanderer mean for my own life?

I find an endorsement of the fact that it is important to be in the company of 'good' people who see through their hearts.

17

With me, in addition to seeing through their eyes, it takes a long time before I can recognise what I am burdened with. However, I don't always run around with my miseries and burdens but rather look for a cool place. I take care of myself, create positive, pleasant experiences for myself.

I can also be the person who meets the wanderer and draws his attention to his "millstone". I sometimes find it difficult to get rid of my own burdens. There is something like the "intolerable easiness of being" (Milan Kundera) in me: as if I would myself find out punctuation the difficult things of life in order to ascertain that they are too difficult for me. I talk here about partnership relations. Of course, I have recently done away with these partnership relations and now I am fine. This can also be compared with the situation in the story: One need not carry about brackish water if a cool, clear stream is flowing along."

Small actions change the world.

**If you are not patient with small things,
you cannot do big things.**

**A small fire which gives you warmth is better
than a big fire which burns you.**

Man lives not even a hundred years but worries for a thousand– Perfectionism can make a person sick

The Perfect Camel

Years ago four scholars were travelling through the Kawir desert with a caravan. In the evening they sat together beside the fire and talked about their experiences. They were all filled with admiration for the camels. They were amazed at their contentment. They admired their strength; and they found their modest patience almost incomprehensible. "We are all masters of the pen," One said, "Let's write about or draw this animal, and so praise and honour the camel." Saying these words, he took a roll of parchment and went into a tent that was lit by an oil lamp. After a few minutes, he came out and showed his work to his three friends. He had drawn a camel just getting up from a resting position. The camel was so well drawn that one would almost think it were alive. The next man then went into the tent and soon came out. He brought a short factual depiction of the advantages that camels bring to a caravan. The third wrote an enchanting poem. Then the fourth man finally went into the tent and forbade the others to disturb him. A few hours later, the fire had gone out, and the others were already asleep. But, from the dimly lit tent, there still came the sound of the scratching of the pen and a monotonous song. The three next day, the three waited futilely for their colleague. Like the cliffs that had closed behind Aladdin, the tent hid the fourth scholar. Finally, on the fifth day, the entrance to the tent opened, and

19

the most industrious of the industrious stepped out, dead tired, with black-rimmed eyes and sunken cheeks. His chin was framed by a stubbly beard. With tired steps and a look on his face as if he had eaten green lemons, he approached the other men. He wearily threw a bundle of parchments onto the carpet. On the outside of the first roll he had written in large letters, "The perfect camel, or how a camel should be ..."

A 37-year-old clerk with compulsions based on excessive order and accuracy tells what effect the story The Wanderer had on him:

At first I wondered how one could drag about so much. But then it occurred to me that many people make their life difficult with so much burden without knowing it. I think I have also burdened myself with too much load.

In my life too, some people have told me that I put too much burden on myself. Although I understand this, I am not able to free myself emotionally from these loads. I am often worried about my son, our business and lots of other things. I would very much like to do what the wanderer did and simply throw away loads, so that I can live without fears and worries, and enjoy my life."

Life has an end, worries don't. (J.Jol)

**A clever man doesn't make all his mistakes alone, but also gives others a chance.
(Winston Churchill)**

Generosity soothes the heart—
Of giving and taking

The Greedy Host

A visitor reached his host's place after travelling a long way, but the host did not offer him food, saying that his stores were empty. The visitor, who saw the rich harvest on the fields through the window, and the feathered birds in the farm, asked his host how much one had to pay to a butcher. He said he intended to slaughter his horse and prepare with its meat a nutritious meal for all. "But how will you then return home?" asked his host. "With your permission, my friend", replied the visitor, "I shall borrow one of your ducks or chickens and ride back home."

A 38-year-old lad with depression due to problems of thriftiness says:

"The story of the wanderer tells us how many unnecessary burdens we drag about with us. It also shows how difficult it is for the wanderer (ourselves) to recognise these burdens. Again and again, other people have to draw his attention to these loads. The story also indicates an inner transformation of the wanderer. First, the boulder: He sees only his hard, tormenting life. Perhaps he can concentrate only on his next step. He does not perceive things around him. The boulder is easily visible to the other people and once it is pointed out to him, it is very easy for the wanderer to throw it away. He feels lighter, he has removed something insignificant from his outer surroundings.

Second, the rotten pumpkin and the heavy iron weights: Again it is another person who draws the attention of the wanderer to his loads. Did these things have any significance for the wanderer in the past? The pumpkin has grown; the chains have bound him to something that was valuable for him. When he is told how much burden these things are for him, he looks a little into himself and admits that he didn't know what he was doing to himself with these things. He cannot remove this load simply by throwing it away from himself. He must shake off the chains and smash the pumpkin. This he does with much more consciousness than in the case of the first load.

Third, the rucksack with sand and the water hose: These are important things for the wanderer. Water is necessary for survival. Here too it is another who tells the wanderer how insignificant these things are. He need not carry sand with him as it lies in large quantities all around him. He would do better to fill the hole with it. And the water in the bar is only getting brackish. There is sufficient fresh water along his path. He must only take a look at his environment to recognise it. The moment he does this he is able to see the heavy millstone around his neck, and recognise it without the help of others. His eyes become free to see the essential things, and he wanders into the evening without burdens. He opens his heart and perceives his environment.

My aim is I must not struggle for anything. I must not justify or assert myself with others."

The world is an interesting book, but it is useless for those who cannot read it.
(Carlo Goldoni)

The art of convincing others–
Developing emotional intelligence

The Power of Persuasion

Once Confucius and his companions stopped for a break on their journey. One of their horses ran away and started grazing on the field of a farmer. This angered the farmer and he detained the horse. A disciple of Confucius, a scholar in the field of persuasion, volunteered to go to the farmer. He held a touching speech before the farmer. But the farmer took no notice of him. A simple man, who had joined then only before requested Confucius, "Let me do the job." He said to the farmer, "You have land here in the west and we have ours in the east. When you come to us in the east where you have no land, your horse may graze on our land. When we come to the west where we have no land, where can our horse graze if not on your field?" On hearing this, the farmer was enthusiastic. He said, "Clear and simple, this is the right way of speaking and not like the man who came before you." He returned the horse. (Narrated by Nossrat Peseschkian)

A 48-year-old manager, who often got angry, was emotionally overexerted and had difficulties in working in a team or persuading the employees. His observation on the wanderer:

"I feel like I am the wanderer on an endless path, without goal. With so many burdens and boulders the wanderer had to master this path and he did not recognise the loads he was carrying! It was the same with me. My father had a recurring

24

illness that took him to hospital often. When my grandmother died on Christmas Day, my mother was left alone to look after me.

Then in the last two years of school there was the pressure of studies, and the unending class quarrels and the trouble with my father. My friends were all from parallel classes, except my best friend Helmut. His father was also ill and therefore we had something in common.

The wanderer was carrying sand with him in a desert full of sand. He was also carrying a water bar although a stream was flowing close by. The sand and the stream are my five friends who met me in the last years of school. I could talk to these friends and share some of my problems with them.

Now the wanderer also had a millstone around his neck due to which he could not walk straight. The millstone is, in my case, the fear that everything comes back. But just like the wanderer, I am going on my way to find a lodging– (my target). My lodging is to become an "ergo-therapist."

It was good for the patient that his performance was recognised by the therapist. After his personal performance was recognised and he could definitely feel this recognition, he was in a position to move forward step by step. The working up was no more negative for him, but rather a step on the way to his own interests and new goals.

It is an art to divide a cake in such a way that everyone believes to have got the largest piece.

The journey to happiness–
Detachment as further development

Once upon a time there was a boy. His name was Hans. Hans was always nice to others and therefore everybody loved him. One day, a man presented him a bar of gold. Hans was happy and started walking home.

(First stanza: "Wandering is the joy of the miller ...")

On his way home, he met a rider with a horse. The rider said, "The horse is very useful. You can ride it over hedge and ditch, move forward as fast as water, and don't have to walk!" Hans exchanged the gold bar for the horse. He was happy that he would not have to walk.

(Second + third stanza: "We learnt it from water ...")

Hans was as fast as the water and the wind. Then he met a farmer with a cow. The farmer said, "Ah Hans, why so fast? I'll give you the cow. It gives milk. You can sit in peace and make cheese out of it. Just give me your horse in exchange. You will see how good it is with a cow." Hans exchanged the horse for the cow and now he walked again quite slowly and comfortably as the stones wander.

(Fourth stanza: "The stones themselves ...")

After going a little ahead, Hans met a man with a grinding machine. He used it to sharpen people's scissors and knives. The grinder saw him and said, "Man, Hans, I'd like to exchange with you. Take my grinding machine. You can earn a lot of money with it." Hans made the exchange and was very happy. But while walking, he felt the grinding machine on his shoulders a bit heavy. So he sat at a well to rest. There it happened: The grinding machine fell into the well. Now, Hans had nothing. Yet he was happy and said to himself, "Ah, how good it is to have nothing! Now I can gladly go home to my mother." Whistling and singing he continued his journey.

(Last stanza: "Oh! wandering, wandering, my pleasure...")

At last he came to his mother. She took him in her arms and said, "Dear Hans, stay with me! Don't go away so far again!" They embraced each other and lived happily ever after. (Grimm)

A 35-year-old woman lived with her 62-year-old mother. The daughter was diagnosed with schizophrenia by many specialists. She had been under medical treatment for many years. Her life history shows that she has not learnt any profession inspite of being sufficiently intelligent. Instead, she always helped her mother in the household work. Mother and daughter were closely associated with each other since the father left the family 28 years ago. The mother had always removed any difficulties in her daughter's way, but at the same time also prevented her independent development. The mother was very intelligent and resolute. An excerpt from a dialogue between mother and daughter:

Mother: Come, the food is ready.
Daughter: Yes mama, I am coming.
Daughter: Mama, the food tastes very good.
Mother: Then eat well!

Two days later:

Mother: You have become quite fat of late. You look almost ugly. You will find it difficult to get a husband. It won't be easy to get a job either.

Daughter: Yes mama, you are right.

The next day:

Mother: Come, the food is ready.

(The daughter eats a little, then puts the spoon down.)

Mother: Why are you not eating? Is the food tasty?

Daughter: No, I am too fat. I want to lose weight.

Mother: You are rude and unthankful. Why have you not combed your hair?

Daughter: I have told you I want to lose weight. You cannot talk me over.

Mother (Cries, touches her heart, breathes heavily): I am finished. I am finished.

The daughter tries to console the mother, and after the mother has calmed down, eats the whole plate. After this scene the daughter eats well every day, so that the mother has no reason to complain. She is obedient. Each time the daughter tries to do something against the wishes of the mother, the latter resorts to sickness in the same way as in the above dialogue. It is clear that the actions of the mother are well-intended. She is worried about the physical well-being of the daughter. This good intention however, seems to be hampered by other tendencies unknown to both of them.

The mother has the following tendencies:

She wants to keep the daughter to herself, all the more since the other two daughters live away from her. From this viewpoint, the attempts of the daughter to become slim were seen as an attempt to find a man, or to take up a job; in other

28

words to move away from the mother. The rejection of food was conceived by the mother as a personal rejection of herself. In order to prevent this, the daughter was made to eat as much as possible. This in turn, strengthened the objective dependence on the mother. Here, under the good intention of the mother, one can see deeply lying unfulfilled desires, expectations, fears, and aggressions. The mother did not wish to be left alone. At the same time, the daughter was to do what the mother wanted.

It is a fact that one remains a child of one's parents for life. This is a relationship that is natural and unavoidable. But often something more is concealed behind it. The parents continue to regard and tutor their children as children even when they have long grown up. They ignore the sense of independence increasing in the children with their development. Every human being needs time for development. He needs it for his physical growth, his psychological differentiation and unfolding in social life. On the other hand, he is also expected to devote time to others. All disturbances in the upbringing can be attributed to an untimely taking-over and unreasonable expectation of roles. Overdemanding, underdemanding and inconsistency are the central causes for this. They manifest themselves especially when the development of the child, the parents and society overlap. The effects increase manifold. Matters seemingly irrelevant, turn into dramatic potentials of conflict.

Underdemanding: The above mentioned case may serve as an example. The capacities of a person are not challenged in accordance with his development.

Overdemanding: A six-year-old child, who had been wrongly sent to school one and a half years earlier, showed deficiencies in learning. An assessment by a pedagogue showed "underdevelopment for his age due to lack of intelligence". An examination of this assessment showed that the child was in fact well developed for his age but the pedagogue had taken the average age of the class into consideration and not the actual age of the child.

Overdemanding does not necessarily lead to a withdrawal of the child. It may also have the effect of an alignment to the demand, and result in precocious behaviour. The five-year-old son of a student couple, whose mother was always employed and whose father studied political science, was initially driven by his father to the kindergarten every morning at about nine o'clock. But since the father used to read till late into the night and wanted to sleep in the morning, he gave the child, some medicines without telling his wife, so that the child slept till eleven o'clock. After this, the father spent some time with his son, as substitute for the kindergarten. He tried to give his son technical, political and philosophical knowledge. The child began, in order to get still more attention from his father, to grasp the things told to him. Finally, he started behaving in accordance with the role his father expected of him. The child was (sensible) and restrained in his behaviour, had little contact with children of his age, and developed strong inhibitions that led to behavioural disturbances.

Inconsistency: The child cannot make use of his capacities uniformly. The child is given tasks which it cannot perform because of age. When the educator notices this, he immediately shows sympathy for the child and withdraws the task. The excessive demand in the beginning puts the child in conflict with self-esteem. Then the reference person gives him an inappropriate possibility of solution by withdrawing. The child will expect difficult problems to be solved by others, without his doing anything. As a result, a consistent problem-solving behaviour will not develop, and the child will not work on a task for a long period. "When I was stuck in a game, my mother said, 'Do something else!'"

A proper upbringing means that the needs of a person are fulfilled in accordance with the stage of development, and not all at once, as in the story.

Special Questions:

With every action we carry out, every capability we develop, we also develop self-confidence which makes us capable of detachment. Detachment means that one can independently establish relationships, separate from a partner and turn to a new partner or the same partner again. The capacity of detachment is here synonymous with personal freedom.

When one has said something politely and honestly to the partner and has justified it sufficiently, one still needs to give him time to take the decision. The right of decision cannot be taken away from him. He takes the decision himself, today, tomorrow, perhaps in the near future. Detachment is not possible for everybody at a definite point of time; one may need more closeness, the other more space.

A person who knows only his partner or his parents has less possibility of getting away from them. Sometimes it does not happen before their death. The capacity of detachment can be acquired like any other capability.

If the capacity of detachment is inadequate, it can happen that the attempt of detachment is immediately suppressed by the attachment or distinction of the reference persons. On the other hand, detachment is sometimes explosive and is synonymous with termination of the relationship.

The detachment of a person from a partner or a group does not necessarily mean termination of the relationship, but rather indicates a restructuring, revaluation and further development of the relationship. When someone detaches himself, he needs not only the readiness for detachment by the reference person, but also an appropriate closeness and space.

Stepwise detachment: Leave the child alone sometimes; let him solve problems independently; allow him to visit others and invite others over; show him closeness so that he gains self-confidence; give him space so that he can act independently and get away from the social circle of the parents; give him jobs to do (send him shopping; let him sort out his things in his own way); show him acceptable forms of detachment as examples. For instance, as parents, leave the child with acquaintances occasionally, even overnight. Do something independent of the partner to ensure a certain level of detachment.

No partnership, no social relationship lasts for ever. One can separate spatially, socially and physically. We must also separate physically after death and this is programmed in our life. Death is also a form of detachment and requires a preparation, just like any other form of detachment and any other capability.

Everything that is round is not a ball– Why one cannot judge others by one's own standards

The Merchant and the Parrot

An oriental merchant had a parrot. One day, the bird overturned a bottle of oil. The merchant got angry and hit the parrot with a stick on the back of the head. After this incident, the parrot, that had earlier shown great intelligence, could not speak any more. It lost the feather on the skull and soon became bald-headed. One day, when it was sitting on the almirah of its master's shop, a bald-headed customer entered the shop. On seeing this customer the parrot got very excited. Flapping its wings, it jumped here and there, cawed, and then, to the surprise of all those present, started speaking. "Did you also overturn a bottle of oil and get a blow on the head because you also don't have hair?" (The Persian poet Rumi, narrated by Nossrat Peseschkian)

A nine-year-old boy called the five-year-old daughter of a guest a monkey. The mother of the girl felt offended because she did not understand the compliment behind this observation. The boy had a keen interest in a television programme in which a monkey played an important role. He was enthusiastic about this monkey and the lively behaviour of the girl reminded, him of this monkey. To him, saying the girl looked like a monkey meant: I like the girl. But the girl's mother had always used the word monkey as an abusive word. She attributed the same motive to the nine-year-old boy.

In the same way, children call their mother, for instance, a cow, their father a horse whereby they have no idea about the insulting character of these expressions. They are however punished for this and are described as impolite. The milk-giving cow is compared with the mother who puts cocoa into it. The father, who is hardly at home due to his work is similar to the workhorse in the fantasy of the child. Why should a child not say what he thinks? After all he learnt to be honest.

To draw conclusion about others based on one's personal beliefs can make understanding easier in some cases, but lead to misunderstanding in other cases.

Seen from the viewpoint of depth psychology this means nothing more than: *My child should achieve what I could not achieve.* In this process, unfulfilled desires, unsatisfied needs and missed experiences are transferred by the adults to the child. The difference between the level of development of the adults and that of the child is deliberately overlooked. As a result of this, the demands of the parents become too much for the child. In this context, one can also understand the words of the little girl who, brought up using anti-authoritarian methods, says: *Mummy, must I play today again what I want?* The antithesis would be: *Mummy, must I play today again what you want?*

The reference persons swing the practices, with which they were themselves raised, to the other extreme so that at least their children and partners can get what they themselves could not get.

A 41-year-old bank manager acknowledged, "My behaviour towards my children has been the exact opposite of what I intended. I took over the methods of my parents, but twisted them by 180 degrees."

A 38-year-old manager in a firm, says, "I always tried to be a good model for my children because I did not want my children to suffer like I did. While doing so, I reached the other extreme and wanted, and want to some extent even today, to make everything hundred per cent perfect."

In most cases however, the projected desire is not commensurate with the level of development and the capacities of the partner. The goal requires certain capabilities that have to be developed step by step. In these cases, one is taking the second step before the first step. The projection of one's own desires and the demand to identify oneself with them, makes the partner and the person himself emotionally overstressed.

Children look at things the way their parents see them. They also *experience* things through identification in a similar manner. Every person can discover in himself elements of behaviour and attitudes which were typical of his parents, friends and relatives. But it often happens that this model becomes independent. One does not think, speak and act as one would do on the basis of one's own conviction, but rather imitates what the model would have done in the similar situation.

The following acknowledgment of a mother is definitely comprehensible for many: "Although I know that every child requires freedom, I get annoyed over the untidiness of my daughter in the same manner as my mother got annoyed over my untidiness. It gets on my nerves that I use the same arguments and words as my mother ..."

This gives rise to a tradition of prejudices and symptoms. The parent's views become the only possible attitude for the child. One can speak of it as a second nature. This second nature can block the access to the first one's own nature.

Broadening of goals

Identification takes place as a mental mechanism and remains unnoticed for most of the time. As the socially most important form of learning, it is a necessary precondition for personality development. But if the identification model is not integrated properly, i.e., if it is taken over rigidly and not developed further in accordance with the prevailing level of personality, it can cause disturbances and conflicts. These are based on the misunderstanding that one does not differentiate between one's own personality and the behaviour patterns of the model. The prerequisite for understanding what another person is thinking or feeling is that we put ourselves in his position. This action can be a projection.

Projection means the transfer of conscious and unconscious expectations, as well as characteristics of one's own personality to the outer world and the social partners. People unknowingly use "projection" to see in others the properties which they possess but do not want to see them in themselves. They see the thorn in others' eyes but not the beam in their own eyes. "Projection" is a systematic dishonesty against oneself and injustice towards the partner. An example of this is an aggressive person. If asked why he attacks others, treats them impolitely and dishonestly, hurts and abuses them, he will reply that he must defend himself because the others are so big and mean and the world is so unjust.

Not everyone who has a bald head, has overturned a bottle of oil.

One can interpret this to mean: Do not judge others by your own standards; ask for the motives.

Question: Tell me, why do you play the piano for five hours every day?

Answer: One must only know what one wants. Question: And what do you want? Answer: The adjacent apartment.

A man accompanied his friend to the railway station. When they reached there, the train was ready for departure. Both the men ran behind the train. One of them succeeded in jumping into the train. The other man doubled up with laughter. When someone asked him the reason, he replied, "Actually I was the one who had to travel by the train."

**The greatest arrogance and the greatest timidity are equal to the greatest self-ignorance.
(Baruch Spinoza)**

Prejudices are based on rumours–
A prejudice has many faces

The Crow and the Peacock

In the palace park, a black crow perched on the branches of an orange tree. Down on the well-tended lawn, a peacock marched about proudly. The crow screeched, "How can one even permit such a strange bird to enter this park? He walks around as arrogantly as if he were the sultan himself. And with those downright ugly feet! And his feathers such a horrible shade of blue! I would never wear a colour like that. He drags his tail around like a fox." The crow stopped and waited silently for a reply. The peacock did not say anything for a while, but then he began to speak with a melancholy smile. "I don't think your assertions correspond to reality. The bad things you say about me rest on misunderstanding. You say I am arrogant because I hold my head up so that my shoulder feathers stick out and a double chin disfigures my neck. In reality, I am anything but arrogant. I know my ugly features, and I know my feet are wrinkled and leathery. This actually bothers me so much that I hold my head erect in order not to see my ugly feet. You see only my ugly parts. You close your eyes to my fine points and to my beauty. Haven't you noticed that? What you call ugly is exactly what people admire in me." (P Ehtesami, Persian poetess, translated and narrated by Nossrat Peseschkian)

The crow in the above story had noticed only the ugly feet of the peacock. The positive features were suppressed under this impression. The concept of ugliness is debatable. Here the ugly feet conceal the other (good) features.

A 63-year-old housewife suffering from sleep disturbances and aggression narrates:

"Earlier I visited many programmes with my husband. On these occasions, it often happened that a well-known professor delivered a lecture. Some long-haired, untidy, young people would sit in a corner and behave uncouthly. So I would be set against them from the very beginning and assume they would make aggressive remarks against the speaker. It never occurred to me to think why these youth act the way they do. Inwardly I would get so agitated that I would often feel sick and I could go over to the boys to bring them to book. Instead , I would behave as usual, so that nobody would notice what was going on inside me. It struck me quite early that I hated any type of aggression in any person although I myself had to struggle so much with it. Now I realise that the reason is that I was brought up almost always in an aggressive atmosphere."

The story narrated at the beginning of this chapter became an example for this patient, who carefully oriented herself to it. She observed that in the same way as the crow had denied the positive features of the peacock, she had seen only the mistakes, conflict areas and trouble spots of other people.

The following example of a 28-year-old mother of an 8-year-old son shows the effect the feelings afflicted with prejudices can have. The boy was brought for psychotherapeutic treatment due to his aggressive behaviour.

"When my son comes to me, in need of loving care, quiet and without aggression, then I think that he is the most loving child in the world. At that time, I love him very much and don't understand how I can sometimes be so strict with him. My feeling of guilt grows and I want to make everything good as quickly as possible. But if he comes to me very aggressive, cheeky and stubborn, then I think what a terrible child I have. I wonder why I deserve such a son?"

Prejudices, no matter whether they are positive or negative, are mainly due to the field of vision which has been restricted by making generalisations. A current capability is emphasised one-sidedly and separated from the personality of the partner. Expectations and attitudes are then linked with this capability.

"You are and will always remain untidy."

"If you lie once, nobody will ever believe you."

"You have always disappointed me; don't try to fool me."

"I have read it myself and it is also true."

"I know myself what is right and what is wrong."

Hatred against groups, races and peoples can be traced, in principle, to this misunderstanding which lies in all generalisations.

"You are nasty to all the people."

"You have never had any time for me."

"You have never been nice to me."

"You always make me wait."

"The rich are exploiters, the poor are failures; the Swiss are very clean; the Bavarians booze; the Scots are miserly; politicians are of bad character; doctors are only interested in earning a lot of money; men want only one thing; all women are snakes ..."

The mechanism of generalisation is used most extensively in making statements about people. And this can be very tragic as the statement of an 8-year-old girl shows: "I am distrustful of everybody. Since my parents have separated, I do not trust any person."

Individual experiences can be generalised to such an extent that the whole way of experiencing God and even the relationship with God are affected by it. An apparently good relationship with God or a total rejection of God are based on this. "If there is a God, then why is there so much injustice in the world?"

Broadening of goals

A mental function, without which we cannot understand our environment is the capability to recognise one event from another and to behave in a similar manner in similar situations. Learning and coping with the environment requires the capability of generalisation. Without it, the individual perceptions and experiences would disintegrate into a host of incoherent events. Without generalisation it is not possible to summarise the perceptions, to form generic terms and finally to think in abstract terms. But this very capability can also lead to a basic type of misunderstanding. The conclusion about one thing based on another contains in it the possibility of false assessment.

If a child has burnt itself on hot oven, it does not touch an oven for a long time, no matter whether it is hot or cold. The protective function of generalisation is evident in this case. But at the same time, this protective function corresponds with the danger that reality is seen only under the aspect of one or more experiences or realisations. From the fact that the oven was hot at one time, one cannot conclude necessarily that it ought to be hot at another point of time. In the relations

41

to oneself and to other people, one tends to make generalisations and draw conclusions from individual experiences about properties, from one property about other properties, and finally from these properties about the whole person.

Typical for generalisation is that one puts emphasis on one area and becomes blind to other areas. Generalisation necessitates narrowing of the field of vision.

Prejudices do not tend to correct themselves but rather go over into other prejudices or swing to the opposite side. People would rather change the world, but not their prejudices. Why is it so difficult to dismantle prejudices? Often people do not notice at all that they have a prejudice. In order not to subject the prejudice to a test and not to let it be questioned, one tries instinctively to avoid discussions that can shake it. But how can a person ever know whether he is making a mistake (in the form of a prejudice) if he never exposes himself to an experience that could bring it to light? How can we be aware of our prejudices if we are not ready to meet others, who have completely different views and characteristics from us?

**It costs nothing to build castles in the air,
but it is very costly to dismantle them.**

**Never believe anything that goes against reason,
without putting it to test.**

If you need a helping hand, look for it at the end of your own arm— Realise your abilities

No one is born a master

A magician presented his art at the court of the sultan. The spectators were filled with enthusiasm. The sultan was also beside himself with admiration. "God, stand by me! what a wonder. What a genius!" His wazir said, "Your Highness, no one is born a master. The art of the magician is the result of his hard work and practise." The sultan wrinkled his brow. The contradiction by the wazir had spoiled his joy at the magician's performance. "You ungrateful man! How can you say that such abilities come with practise? It is as I say: Either one has talent, or one doesn't have it." Disparagingly he looked at the wazir and shouted, "You don't have it in any case. Go to prison. There you can think over my words. You will get a calf as your companion in the prison, so that you are not lonely and have someone like you around you." From the very first day, the wazir started lifting the calf. Every day he carried it over the stairs of the prison tower. Several months passed. The calf grew into a massive bull and the power of the wazir grew with daily practise. One day, the sultan remembered his prisoner. He ordered him to be brought before him. On seeing him he was overwhelmed with astonishment. "God, stand by me what a wonder. What a genius." The wazir, who was carrying the bull in his arms, replied with the same words as earlier, "Your Highness, no one is born a master.

You had given me this animal as a favour. My power is the result of my hard work and practise."

The king saw an extraordinary person in the magician–a person who possessed certain special powers that could not be matched by any other person. For him, the performances of the magician were out of this world, and it was for this reason that he also idolised him.

A child lost his sight in the left eye due to a car accident. From the medical point of view, his eyesight could not be restored. This was a fact that he would have to come to terms with. It was interesting to note, however, that in this case, the child developed quite normally despite his handicap, but the mother, who had driven the car, could not really come out of the shock.

We often tend to overlook the obvious fact that a person's upbringing can influence the way one's inherent deficiencies affect one's life – positively or negatively.

A famous historical example of the possibilities that exist despite inherent deficiencies is that of the deaf, dumb and blind girl, Hellen Keller. This girl, who was once a helpless, animal-like creature, grew up to be a highly sophisticated, admirable personality. This was made possible by the patience of her governess. She saw in her not only the deficiencies, which could have led one to lose hope, but also the hidden talents that were independent of the physical deficiencies. Even though she could not see, hear, or speak, she still had the sense of touch. It was this that came to her rescue as also her hands and face which were her means of expression.

There are two possibilities to deal with inherent deficiencies in a helpful manner. One could be either try to influence the deficiency itself; for example, through an operation, through medicines or through exercises or one could try to shift the focus to the other capabilities or talents that exist besides the deficiency. Even a handicapped child can develop qualities like discipline, cleanliness, politeness, ability to perform and other such constructive capabilities, if handled with a lot of patience and consistent care.

The experiences of the past are a part of fate that cannot be changed. What is once done cannot be undone. The only thing one can change is the attitude towards the happening or experience. In the same way one, cannot avert the fate that has been determined for him. What one can, however, do, is to change the way one deals with it. Our view of the present – whether it is diverse or restricted – is dependant on this very attitude. Which perspective an individual chooses to follow is in itself a sort of conditional fate, which is partially dependant on the type of one's upbringing.

It is not only the attitude of the person of reference to the child and the partner that the misunderstanding of the concepts of "conditional and definite fate" gains importance. It is also reflected in one's attitude towards oneself: "I am an unlucky person; this is my fate. It has always been so and will always remain so." This expression is subject specific. The concerned person identifies himself with certain characteristics and abilities to perform and sees no other possibilities. The expression: "I am unlucky" is fundamentally different from: "I had a stroke of bad luck." The latter concerns itself with individual occurrences, which are not clubbed or interchanged with the personality per se.

"I had an accident and then I always got into an accident. I am unlucky."

"I believed that I could not learn. Before any exam in my profession I would always say to myself: 'You will not be able to do this!' and I could not do it."

45

"It is always easier for others to do things; for example to make friends with women. I have always found it difficult to make friends with them; no one talks to me."

"My mother was very apathetic in nature; I got it from her. One can't do anything about that; it is the way it is."

"What have I achieved in life? When I look around me I see someone has built a house, another has a nice wife, and I have absolutely nothing."

These examples clearly mark out the distinction between *defined* and *conditional* fate. A defined fate is one which is inevitable and cannot be avoided. For instance, every being is born and dies one day. There is no way one can avoid this fact of life. Besides this question of life and death, there is another question that often bothers man – the question of whether there is a life after death, which forms the origin and the aim of all existence, which is the essence of the creator himself. Every human being confronts this question; there is no exception.

The conditional fate, on the other hand, is one which has its own history behind it. It is one which could have been avoided and the means to change which lie in our hands. And this is precisely the kind of fate that can be related to all of the above examples.

The following example further clears the distinction between the defined and conditional fate. The fate of a candle is defined, in that it is meant to burn itself out. This is a fact, which cannot be changed. Conditional fate, however, can be reflected in the following occurrence: While the candle is still burning, a gush of wind comes and blows it out. This is an example of conditional fate, as there were enough means to avoid this particular situation.

Broadening of goals

Besides the problems that have been dealt with under the topic of defined fate, all other occurrences come under the head of conditional fate. This means that the upbringing of a child or any other person (even that of the individual himself) can shape his or her life in a positive manner if done properly. If, however, this does not prove to be successful and there are deficiencies or uncalled for developments that occur, one can normally overcome them if they are recognised at the right time i.e., they can be cured if timely detected. Other deficiencies, however, that are dependent on, and are a result of certain occurrences, cannot be cured through scientific means. In this case, one has to accept the deficiencies and develop a positive attitude towards them. This would help in the development of the other capabilities of the person at least.

It is impossible for someone to do everything. This is a fact that cannot be refuted but at the same time it is also true to say that everyone has the potential to develop a lot of capabilities in oneself, the only constraint being time and space. Once these constraints are taken care of, one can achieve his true potential.

A good possibility for that would be the following: Do not help a child or even your partner in areas where you feel that they can cope on their own. Wait till they do the work themselves, even though they may do it wrong. It is only in this way that step-by-step learning is made possible. It is only in this way that a person learns to be independent and builds confidence in himself.

Nothing big has ever been achieved without enthusiasm. (Ralph W. Emerson)

Miracles happen only to those who believe in them.

In order to see, you must open your eyes.

In order to discern, you must close them and think. One cannot add days to life, but one can add life to a day.

Hope is the only possession that is common to all human beings. (Thales von Milet)

What I don't know does not bother me!–
The ability of asking the right questions to yourself and others

The Half-truth

Prophet Mohammed came with his follower to a city to preach. Soon another follower came to him and said, "Sir, it is useless to preach here, as nobody wants to learn. You will not be able to make any difference sir." The Prophet answered softly, "You are right." Thereafter, another person came to him and said, "Sir, you are in a happy city. The people here look forward to the right teaching and would open their hearts to your words." Mohammed smiled and said again, "You are right." The first follower was shaken. "Oh Sir!" said the follower. "You told me that I was right and to the second, who contradicted me, you said the same. Black can never be white." Mohammed perception?, One of them sees the dark side, while the other sees the bright side. Would you say that either of them was wrong? Are people not both good and bad at the same time? None of the two said anything wrong to me. What they said was only incomplete". (Retold by Mr Nossrat Peseschkian).

A major part of all the function of the soul and the interpersonal relationships are dictated by the attitudes and behaviour of people, the origins and motives of which are not known. Due to these certain processes take place, which are not intended and the consequences of which are undesirable.

The couple B resorted to psychotherapy as they had problems with their marriage. Mr B, 42 years old and Mrs B, 34 years old, both academicians, complained about family tensions, which had arisen in the last few years, even though they had had a good marriage till then. In their sessions, they always spoke about difficulties with their children, whereby their nine-year-old son held the central position. As the youngest of three siblings, he had built a strong attachment to the mother. In the last few years the father had very little time to spend with the child due to his work. Whenever they met, the son would come out with a whole list of wishes, which the father could not fulfill. The son would then turn to his mother who would appease him by spending more time with him. This worked as an incentive. The situation came to such extremes that the mother turned into a lawyer for her son and there were often confrontations among the parents due to this. This turned into a pattern. "I will pester my father with wishes till the time he refuses to fulfill them. Then I will go to my mother. She will put herself on my cause and spend a lot of time with me. Thereby I would have an edge over my siblings."

The function of the unconsciousness can be explained through the following example: After we eat there are certain processes that are triggered off in our body. We are not aware of these processes until the time a deficiency takes place and pain and discomfort act as a signal of the same. This is similar to interpersonal relationships. How often do we catch ourselves doing something which we did not intend to do? For example, even though we know that punishment is not the best way of bringing up a child and impatience could only result in us losing our temper, we often lose control on the smallest of issues and throw our principles out of the window. Thereafter we repent. This was the case with this mother.

"Sometimes I do something which I later regret and which also is against my principles. I always get angry with my daughter on trivial issues, even though I resolve every day to be nice to her..."

The actual capabilities play a special role as the contents of the unconsciousness. The imbalances in the patterns of the actual capabilities are mostly considered normal and they therefore do not enter the consciousness. Even then they are full of strong feelings and in a way lead their own life, the consequences of which affect relationships with other people. Experiences which lead to a clash between the actual capabilities and the outside world can be suppressed; they disappear from the consciousness. One does not remember them even though they are stored at the back of the mind. We can define this procedure as suppression. The experiences that have not been processed develop their own dynamic and often find expression in dreams, thoughts, speech, and in actions.

Special questions:

Does it happen often that you lose your temper over what you have done (situations)?

Do you completely distance yourself from a person who betrays you (situations)?

Does it happen sometimes that you find qualities in yourself that are also there in your partner or your parents?

Do you consider the problems and difficulties of your partner as your own?

Does it happen that you vent your anger on the children or your partner even though they are not at fault (situations and content)?

How do you feel when you hear of accidents, catastrophes or deaths?

Do you dream often, and if yes, of what and how do you feel at that time?

Does it happen often that you forget something or say something that you did not actually intend to say?

Does it happen often that you repeat your mistakes (situations and content)?

Can you concentrate well or do you have problems with it (situations)?

Are you of the opinion that the unconsciousness has an influence on your behaviour and experience (situations)?

One who wants to have something, must also give something. (Martin Luther)

Everyone has wisdom; it is just that some people gain it before others.

"One is wealthy when one has plenty"–
How much is essential?

The Clever Doctor

Once upon a time there was lady in the Orient who was so fat that she could not walk. One day she decided to go to a doctor in order to get medicine that would reduce her fat. She went to the doctor's house. When she came there, the doctor told her to take a seat and asked her how she was. The lady replied, "Oh thank you. I am doing pretty well. I have come here for a check-up." He asked, "What problem do you have?" The lady replied, "I want you to give me some medicine to reduce my weight." The doctor said, "But I must consult the Oracle first, so that I can check which medicine would be suitable for you. Go home for the time being. Come tomorrow and I will give you the answer." The lady thanked the doctor and went home. She went again on the following day to see the doctor. The doctor said. "My dear lady, I have consulted the book and found that you will be dying in the next seven days. Therefore, I don't think that you need any medicine." The lady got very scared when she heard these words. She went back home, ate nothing, drank nothing and was very sad. Due to this, she lost a lot of weight. Seven days passed by but she did not die. Then she went back to the doctor and said to him, "Today is the eighth day and I am still alive." The doctor asked, "But are you fat or thin?" She said, "I am thin. I lost all my weight because of the fear of dying!" The

doctor went to her. "This was precisely the medicine, the fear."
And the lady went back home.

I narrated this story to a 32-year-old heavily overweight lady who was suffering from fear and depression. Besides, she also described herself as a "wanderer".

"I often feel as if I am a wanderer. I am burdened, tired, but I am unable to see the reason. I feel burdened, for example, when I feel ashamed of myself in front of other people. There are certain things which are important for me and I feel that I have to justify myself. Sweets that have caused my weight problem are also a necessity sometimes. There are a lot of things I own like CDs, books, and household articles that clutter my house. I am ashamed of this when people come over to visit me. But I am, at the same time, very proud of my possessions and feel very comfortable the way I am. Besides, one also needs these things from time to time. The household articles make the housework easier, the food stocks come handy at the time of cooking and so on. Even when we are travelling, I often have things which people otherwise do not carry along. I love books and I buy them all the time. Earlier I was a voracious reader, but unfortunately, I do not have the concentration or the time to read these days. Besides, I also have a guilty feeling when I am reading something, as I should instead be studying. Therefore, I often leave the book unread."

"My CDs are also very important to me. Actually there is always music playing in my house, as I believe that music helps in enhancing the sense of well-being."

"I love to go shopping and to use the things that I buy. I could do with more money and space! But the requirement just seems to keep increasing!"

"Some people do not understand others as they have different priorities in life. People spend money on different things in life. For spending on the latest car or on designer clothes is a waste of money. These options are not available to me, and therefore I try and make do with smaller purchases."

"I vaguely remember a story where a rich person was robbed of all his wealth. Later a poorer person told him that he (the poor person) could enjoy his life without any tensions. This can be true but I also feel that luxurious possessions make life more comfortable. For me it is also difficult to decide as to which possessions I can do without! I am so attached to all of them!"

"The aim can therefore not be to throw away the burden, which, as it is, is a matter of perception. I do not want to do away with the burden. The aim cannot be recognised."

If we follow the history of a deficiency, we can find connections till the very day in life and further back in time when the mother and child were one biological unit. Here we can find the factors which lead to an illness not only in the form of toxic metabolic disorders, but also in the psychosocial processes such as the attitudes of the parents towards the child, in their relationships to one another and in the possibilities which the parents grant their children. A child, when born, comes not only with his own possibilities of development and capabilities in the world, but is also influenced by the parents and the environment, which affects the development of his capabilities to a large extent. With this the potential for conflicts, the concepts and patterns of the conflict resolution are determined, which later prove themselves to be either useful or not.

The concept of *self-help* is not new to the field of medicine. There are diet charts, fitness training programmes and self-control techniques in the field of internal medicine. Under this type of treatment, the patient helps himself under the guidance of the doctor. This help has lately become an essential part of internal medicine as also preventive medicine. In the same manner as diet charts are prepared differently for diabetic patients, liver patients and patients with stomach problems as per their disease and their specific reports, behaviour programmes can also be developed for psychosocial conflicts. When, for example, one's partner or friend is unfaithful, one can react in many ways. One could resort to alcohol or drugs and search for a better world through their help, or one could take revenge and become unfaithful. But, one could also solve this problem in a constructive manner. The suitable alternative is normally chosen from one's own repertoire of possible solutions that one has learnt over the years and from one's own world of creativity.

We do not face a shortage of time; instead we have a lot of time, which we do not use.

One needs much more strength to accept the truth than to defend a mistake.
(George Christoph Lichtenberg)

"One can stand on one's position, but should not remain sitting on it"– When traditions become rigid

The Magician

The mullah, a preacher, wanted to get some nuts for his wife, because she had promised to cook him Fesenjan, a dish prepared with nuts. In the joy of anticipating his favourite dish, the mullah reached deep into the nut jar and grabbed as many nuts as he could reach with one hand. When he tried to pull his arm out of the jar, it got stuck. As hard as he twisted and pulled, the jar would not release his arm. He cried, groaned, and cursed and as a mullah really shouldn't. But nothing helped. Even when his wife took the jar and pulled on it with all her strength, nothing happened. His hand remained stuck in the neck of the jar. After many futile attempts, they called in their neighbours for help. Everyone followed, with great interest, this drama which was being played out in front of them. One of the neighbours took a look at the situation and asked the mullah how he had got himself into such a fix. With a pathetic voice and moans of desperation, the mullah told of the mishap. His neighbour said, "I will help you if you do exactly as I say." The mullah replied quickly, "I promise to do everything you say, if you will just free me from this terrible jar." The neighbour continued, "Then shove your arm further into the jar." This seemed strange to the mullah, for why should he put his arm further into the jar when he wanted to get it out of there? But he did as he was told. The neighbour advised, "Now open your hand, and drop the nuts you holding." This request upset the mullah. After all, he wanted the nuts for his favourite dish, and now he was supposed to just drop them. Reluctantly, he followed his succourer's instructions. The man now said, "Make your hand into a fist, and pull it slowly out of the jar." The mullah did this, and lo and behold, he pulled his hand effortlessly out of the jar. But still he wasn't completely satisfied. "My hand is free now, but where are the nuts?" At that the neighbour took the jar, tipped it over, and let as many nuts roll as the mullah needed. Wide-eyed and open-mouthed, the mullah watched and inquired, "Are you a magician?" (Persian story)

A 27-year-old, chemistry laboratory assistant, and daughter of a doctor, suffered from depression and fear. It struck her that she showed very little initiative of her own, and was lost in thoughts of unrealistic wishes and imaginations of the future. But she could not manage what she expressed as, "Taking control of her life." She described one of her very acute problems as: "I believe that my parents would love to see me married and with children. Recently they have been expressing their wish for grandchildren very often. They imply that am I getting older, but so are they. But I would not like to marry, just to do them a favour. My parents would love to see me marry a doctor, who would take over my father's practice. Then I would have to shift to my parents' house with my partner, which would probably solve a few problems for them.

A partnership, which is considered 'generations duty, leads to the understanding that after a certain age, one must get married and have children. Parents often act as a driving force behind it. They want their sons and daughters to have spectacular wedding parties and want to spoil their grandchildren thereafter. For such weddings, especially in oriental cultures, hundreds of people are invited. The marriage ceremony becomes the aim of life.

A 'generations' duty can seldom be linked with business interests. A son-in-law must take over the business; hence the daughter is allowed to marry only such man who has experience in the family's line of business. Thus, she would carry out the generations duty, as well as fulfill her father's wish.

Three reactions on tradition:

In every relationship and partnership, the aspect of 'tradition' does come forth. At times, they are the expectations, setting of tasks, and wishes, which a person has as an answer to his history of development and sphere of tradition. And at times they are that of the partners'. Both the worlds of traditions clash because of their different contents and goal projections. So the question arises: how well can these worlds harmonise with the new conditions? Thus, we can describe the three forms of associations with tradition. In every case, the possibilities of combinations, which arise due to the differences in the conception of traditions (transcultural aspect), need consideration.

The mummified type: The relationship with tradition is good. Tradition is the guiding line of life. One adopts the norms and rules, which were valid in the previous generations, holds on to them firmly and also substitutes them, if the conditions, under which they were once valid, are changed. This conservative association with tradition gives certainty to the orientation of the plan of life, offers a clear viewpoint, prevents the feeling of insecurity, and grants these only as a prize of rigidity, fixation and inflexibility.

The revolting type: The person turns away categorically from the old traditions and prefers not be involved in it at all. As he gives up on the traditional accomplishment strategies, he has the opportunity of discovering new, own and also contemporary possibilities of solutions. Without the security granted by the tradition, he tries to shoulder the total responsibility for the partnership, alone or together with the partner. The rewards for it are insecurity, over-expectation, social isolation and an illusion. This type is usually the outcome of protest against family traditions, which belong to the same social class or cultural circle. The person lands up searching for new solutions under the spell of other traditions. What was considered as a revolution against tradition is actually responsible for the substitution of traditions.

The indifferent type: The person wants to hold on to the traditions of his family, but at the same time wants to be freed from them. The situation of competition between the family of origin and one's own partnership is most of the time responsible for solidarity conflicts. One wants the new, but does not want to set the old free. Now and then, integration is achieved, especially when the new and the old world are not very different and when the partner is ready for a compromise. But when the indifferent gets caught between the offers of his families' traditions and the demands of his partner, and when he is expected to unite the incompatible through his duties, it is the beginning of a very typical suffering for him. He is torn to pieces, even mentally. He gets divided into the 'brave child' of his parents, as well as of his independent partner. He wants to please everyone, but is unable to do that, when misfortune prevails.

Broadening of goals:

Mummified model proves to be occasionally successful. An example for this would be the Islamic movement of the states of the Middle East. Here, threats of religious-social values are resorted to those who oppose the Islamic tradition. Other religions and values are then openly suppressed and prosecuted.

Special questions:

To which type one belongs is not a decision of free will. Now and then one notices, how one reacts, when one starts to observe oneself and to differentiate the observations. Most of the traditional obligations, which are further passed on as 'generation's duty,' are interlinked with the feeling of self-worth. One identifies oneself with these and makes them a part of oneself. It is related to considering the aspect of tradition as positive and freeing it from the emotional involvements through sequential feelings, blame-reproaches and fear of separation. To help in dealing with this, are a few questions that can be asked:

> To which type do I belong, with the problem, that I am facing at this moment?

> Which position does my partner represent?

> What tradition-related content does it have (order, cleanliness, trust, performance duties etc.) and what does it mean for us?

> Which possibilities does the concept of tradition allow with regard to social relationships? Which are the ones promoted and which social relationships are ignored or blocked?

> Which instruments in our framework of concept of traditions are available and how can we sensibly expand our capability to free ourselves gradually, step-by-step from traditions?

"One should not throw old habits out of the window all at once, but accompany them to the door, like you would accompany your guest."

A mother thinks highly of an anti-authoritative upbringing. And as the first child was born a neighbour asked, "Is it a boy or a girl?" The mother's reply: "Our child should be allowed to think about it later!"

Don't let yourself be impressed by any carter, who would say to you, "Dear friend, I have been doing it this way for twenty years!" One can also do something incorrectly for twenty years. (Kurt Tucholosky)

A habit is a rope. We add a thread to it every day, until finally we cannot open it at all (let go of it).

There are many copies but few originals, among human beings – Discover the uniqueness

Lame Comparisons

Once a cobbler, who suffered from severe pain and was almost near his death, went to a doctor. The doctor made many efforts, but did not find any recipe that would help. The patient asked fearfully, "Isn't there anything that could save me now?" The doctor replied, "I do not know of any other way." To this the cobbler said, "If nothing is going to help me, then I have a wish to make. I would love to have a stew of two kilos of broad beans and one litre of vinegar." The doctor shrugged his shoulders resignedly. "I don't think this will work, but if you feel it will you can try it out." The whole night the doctor kept waiting for news of the cobbler's death. But to the doctor's amazement, the cobbler was full of life and healthy the next morning. So he wrote in his diary: Today a cobbler came to me for whom there was no way left. But two kilos of broad beans and one litre of vinegar helped him. After a while, the doctor was called upon by a severely ill tailor. In this case too the doctor did not have a remedy. Being an honest person, he confessed to the tailor. The tailor begged, "Don't you really know of any other possibility?" The doctor gave it a thought and said, "No, but not before long, a cobbler had come to me. He was suffering from something similar. Two kilos of broad beans and one litre of vinegar were of

*help to him." "If nothing works, then I shall give it a try",
said the tailor. He ate the beans and one litre of vinegar, and
the next day he was dead. In relation to this the doctor wrote
in his diary: Yesterday a tailor came to me. But nothing was
of help to him. He ate two kilos of broad beans with vinegar
and he died. What was good for the cobbler, was not good
for the tailor.*

A 32-year-old mother, who suffered from hysterical fear
and had problems related to the entire field of justice, reports
the following:

"When I am angry with something, then I say something
like this to my daughter: 'Look at your brother, how patient
he is and how he plays so well with his Lego. And you just
keep fooling around like a five-year-old!' To my son I say:
'Your sister, though she is just six, has already stayed alone
or sometimes even does some shopping for me. You behave
like a baby and keep hanging on to my skirt. I keep telling
each child what the other one is good at. I have been doing
this for so long, that they have started hating each other."

This is a typical case for the child's uniqueness often being
misunderstood. Trial by comparison often fails. Consider just
one capacity. However, it is necessary to take into account a
person's uniqueness. The achievement system of our
civilisation, beginning in school and continuing into
occupation, rests on the principle of comparability. Precisely
this leads us to thinking carefully about things. Everyday
experience shows that although human beings have certain
similarities, people differ from one another in countless
particulars. These differences arise mainly with respect to
areas like, the body, environment and time.

Uniqueness and the body: In spite of all the regulations
and legalities, which determine the science of anatomy,

physiology, pharmacy, and biochemistry for the construction and functioning of the human body, professionals of these sciences themselves reject certain principles on grounds of their not taking into account the uniqueness of humans. This can be proved especially by their deviations from the statistical norms, which however do not come under the term of disease.

A conclusion which can be drawn from this is: The type and amount of a medicine are different for different individuals. The individuality is seen in the metabolism and nutrition. While some people are stimulated after having the pleasure of a cup of coffee and cannot sleep after having a cup of tea in the evening, the intake of coffee does not influence the sleeping habits of some people at all. The human nervous system is an exemplary example of individuality and uniqueness. The brains in humans differ from each other in their sizes, mass and weight. One can claim that there are no two humans with the same brain. These anatomical facts also reflect in the individual experiences. Surveys regarding tactile senses such as sensitivity to heat, cold and pain show that every human being reacts differently to the corresponding stimuli. In other words, everyone experiences the world in his own way.

Uniqueness and the environment: The possibilities of variations in bodily and sensory aspects arises when one takes the environment into consideration. The environment affects every individual, every day and every night. The way in which parents treat their child, how much patience they summon up, which position the child has among the siblings – the eldest, the youngest or 'sandwich' child – influences childhood development. Kindergarten, school and the interaction with children of the same age, play a very important role. Later, professional opportunities, choice of profession, experiences with a partner and other human relationships, religious or social convictions, have an affect on the development.

The varied development of a person is based on uniqueness of capabilities on one hand and influence of the environment on the other.

Children are different:

Some children start questioning earlier than the others. Some develop more patience and intensity for questioning, while some question less.

Some children are interested in fairytales and are more eager to listen to them than others.

Some children develop a lively imagination, while some may stick to reality.

There are children, who during their course of development develop an intensive emotional relationship with one of their parents.

One child may prefer to play with his siblings; the other may prefer to play alone, while a third may play in the company of others.

Such differences are also observed in adulthood.

Uniqueness and time: People and the environment they inhabit are dependant on another factor called time. Time makes sure that people change. But the idea of uniqueness should not serve every time to hide all the disturbances in development. Therefore the development of a person can be understood only when one compares the uniqueness with the progress of development, which is described by developmental psychology and developmental physiology.

Singularity is uniqueness and is dependant on time. For example, when a child tells a lie, it depends on the behaviour of the parents. Only with time can the consequences be seen in the later development of the child. The behaviour of the child, when seen with the time-dimension, determines the singularity: the child may show some different behaviour tomorrow, day after tomorrow or next year in a different environmental situation. If the singularity is misunderstood, then a situation of uniqueness is blamed, and one confuses the concrete-situative behaviour of the child with his character. From this, a parent can understand the striking features in behaviour differently. The capability to go beyond the present is the capability to accept a person who annoys you. One has the flexibility to handle a new situation, which looks at the corresponding old situation with a different perspective.

Broadening of goals:

The possibilities of changing human behaviour are relatively high. A child is not condemned for what it is at that moment. This is true for physical complaints as well as mental disturbances. Even then, the possibilities of changing have their limit with respect to time.

As every human possesses uniqueness of body and the experiences of his environment, he is less likely to be affected by others or affect others. This is applicable for explanations and conclusions like:

"The hunter did not harm me, why should it harm my child?" (42-year-old lawyer)

"My parents have had no time for me. But I have still made my life. I see no reason why the problems of my child can be related to that I have less time for him." (45-year-old construction industrialist)

"My friend drinks more alcohol than I do. Then why should it harm me?" (24-year-old student)

"I have given the medicine, which proved to be good for me, to my friend." (32-year-old housewife)

"All the male members of the family have become engineers. It is incomprehensible why our youngest would like to study arts." (44-year-old engineer)

One needs to recognise the special and individual strengths and capacities of other people and to support their development. Many people are practically skilled and others possess abstract capabilities. Many show organisational skills, while others prove to be successful in the artistic areas. Thus there are sufficient possibilities in which one can develop one's special capabilities.

The work of the guardian is similar to that of a gardener, who nurtures different types of plants. One plant loves the rays of the sun, the other the cool shadows; one loves the banks of a river, the other the arid mountain peaks, one prospers best on sandy surfaces, the other in thick mud. Everyone should get proper care suited to his type, otherwise the garden remains unsatisfactory. (From the Bahai writings).

Learn to differentiae between and uniformity uniqueness.

Love is like a glass that breaks if held too loose or too tight— Love and justice

The Division of Labour

"I can't take it any more. The tasks are like mountains which I can no longer move. I have to wake up early in the morning, wake you up, straighten the house, clean the carpets, watch the children, go shopping at the bazaar, cook your beloved rice dishes in the evening, and finally pamper you at night."
Thus spoke a wife to her husband. Chewing on a drumstick, the latter expressed his simple opinion: "So what? All women do the same as you. You have it good, you know. While I take the responsibility, you sit around the house." "If you could just help me a little bit," asked the woman. In a moment of generosity, the husband finally agreed to the following suggestion: While the wife would take responsibility for everything that happened in the house, he would assume the tasks outside of the house. For a long time, the couple lived happily with this division of labour. One day, after busily shopping, the husband was sitting in a cafe and smoking a water pipe with satisfaction. A neighbour suddenly stormed in and shouted excitedly, "Come quickly, your house is on fire." Savouring the water pipe, the man took it out of his mouth and said with remarkable equanimity, "Be so kind as to tell my wife, for after all she is responsible for everything that happens in the house. I am only responsible for external affairs."

"Though I knew that it would not work out well, I married my husband." Why? The woman who is 26-year-old now, got to know her later husband when she was 18-year-old, shortly after her studies began. Both stayed in the same hostel, on the same floor, and both of them felt equally alone in the unknown surroundings. They went out together, went to each other's rooms, did not want to spend the nights alone, got used to each other, stayed together till the end of their studies, could hardly dare to think of separation, and finally got married, though there was much to be desired in this relationship. In their first meeting, itself she was angry with him as he had got a drink for himself and had not bothered to get a drink for her. Later she was burdened as he made her pay for everything and took her for granted. Soon she noticed that he hardly had any interest in sports, and that he did not even own a pair of swimming trunk, as he did not want to swim. But all this did not stop the development of their relationship and their subsequent marriage. They did get married, as she later says, so secure and fateful, "Just like the Amen in the church."

Examples of over-emphasis on justice:

I do all the outside chores so that you can look after the house and children.

"You have no time for me now, so henceforth even I shall not have time for you."

"You have no time for me now; hence I shall search for someone who has time for me."

"Today you are professionally successful, you have cared so much for us, so I will love you for this."

"Now that you have shown a good performance in school, you may go for the movie today."

"You have behaved well in front of the guests; hence you can stay awake a bit longer and watch TV."

For justice, equality and comparability are very important factors. This knowledge was the basic principle of the legislation, of Hamurabi (1686-1728 BC): Punishments act as safeguards. They broaden the understanding of the people and work as the means of precaution from repetition of mistakes. Justice, a very important principle, which also rules our legislation, acts as a very decisive factor in the different forms of upbringing. Justice, when made absolute, in the relationship between partners, leads to a vicious circle, in which one injustice is followed by another. Marriage becomes a living hell. When justice is considered by most of the people as a symbol of consequence, it appears to be quite unstable when experienced. An action is judged in connection with the experiences. One's value system, previous imaginations and wishes remain affected by it.

Examples for over-emphasis on love:

"I will always be there for you and give you everything that I have, irrespective of what you give me."

"I have confidence in you, and trust you."

These statements are statements of love. Love is a sign of positive emotional affection and encompasses the person as a whole. One does not cling to certain qualities, capacities, and peculiarities, but rather regards the bearer of these attributes. "I love you, because you are you."

For the relationship between partners, this orientation is advantageous in many cases. The upcoming problems are played up but apparent conflicts are avoided. In extreme cases, love loses its control of reality and becomes detached from concrete conditions. One speaks of 'monkey love' in such cases. In the case of justice, one has expectations, which are to be met in the present. However the attitude towards expectations in love are not time bound. One is patient and hopes that at some point of time, love (the devotion) for the partner will be rewarded when it is recognised by the environment or by God:

> "When my son behaves in an indisciplined fashion, I do not see it at all."

> "My husband has very little time. But I don't tell him about it, as I would not like to hurt him. Irrespective of what he does, I still love him."

If the principle of justice rules in the upbringing situations, conflicts, are sought out actively–one criticises. In extreme cases, the principle of justice leads to instances such as, children being beaten, youth being expelled by parents, breaking up of friendships and marriages. One simply does not want to know about one's child, if he does not do something that is expected of him: "You do not want to obey, so you have nothing to look forward to from us."

If the principle of love dominates, it poses a threat of an opposite effect. Conflicts smolder behind masks of patience and politeness, without giving it an opportunity of letting off some steam from time to time. If conflicts are not sorted out step-by-step, it may lead to explosive outbreaks. Such people swallow everything; very often they become their children's servants. Something very minor can set of a major reaction in such people. The basic principle holds true: Everything or nothing. A mother, who was otherwise peaceful, got an unexpected raving fit and mistreated her children in case of an insignificant offence. A father, who had never beaten six-year-old son, beat the child so hard, when he did not wish to eat some food. A woman left the house after her husband forgot their anniversary.

Not only do the just and loving people exist, justice and love merge so well, that very often the conflict-partner cannot decide which of them he actually favours. Let's imagine a fight between a married couple. The wife forgets to go to the bank to do some work on behalf of her husband. The husband is annoyed and shouts at her. One cannot rely on you at all, he says. With this obvious outbreak of feelings, immediately the feeling of guilt-consciousness arises. I should not have shouted at her, he thinks. As he sees his wife washing the utensils in the kitchen, he ties an apron and starts helping her with the drying of dishes and whispers, "I did not mean it that way." On the other hand, love can be converted to strong justice, when expectations concerning love and emotions are not met. The most difficult thing in such situations is that, the partner has no idea of the shift in his ideas.

Broadening of goals:

Living together (human ties) and upbringing of children are based on justice and love. But principles can lead to social and mental conflicts, if one of them dominates the other; if one is underrated or if both are not in cooperation with the dimension of time.

It makes sense to make demands of the partner, in terms of justice. He even expects these demands. When he makes a mistake, however, it is necessary to distinguish between inadequate accomplishment and the person himself. This means: I accept you the way you are, even if you have just made a mistake in this area. I know that you can learn from your mistakes and I will learn from my own.

Learn to differentiate between love and justice
Special questions on love and justice:

Justice
It is the capability to carefully consider interests with respect to oneself and others. One finds treatment unjust, when personal liking and disliking dictate over practical decision-making. The social aspect of this actual capability is social justice. Every person has a sense of justice. The way in which parents treat a child, how just they are with him, with his siblings and with each other, determines the frame of reference of justice for an individual.

Who gives more importance to justice amongst you? (Justice or injustice and against whom?)

Do you think your partner is just (to the children, parents-in-law, fellow human beings and himself)?

How do you react when you are not treated justly (in your profession, in the family etc.)?

Have you ever faced problems related to injustice? Has someone else been preferred to you?

Who between your parents pays more attention to justice to you or to your siblings (situation)?

It is the capability to have a positive and emotional relationship, which can act according to a series of objects of varied gradation. Love does not contain any uniform behaviour. One has the ability to love someone and the ability to behave in such a manner, to be loved by someone. A general suggestion such as, "Give the child more love!" is not very helpful. An explanation of the area in which there is a love-deficit and the emotional relationship attached is a better way to tackle the love-justice dilemma. The most important forms of expression of love in upbringing are: model, patience and time.

Do you accept yourself (your own body)?

Which of you is more inclined to accept the other partner?

Would you prefer to have your partner just for yourself?

Do you feel insecure or awkward in a large group?

What would you have done if your partner had professional and financial problems? Would you still like to be with him?

What would happen if you suddenly had to live at subsistence level?

Can you handle household matters individually without your partner, or do you depend on him?

Were you as a child, and later as an adolescent accepted by your parents?

Were people at home generous or sparing when it came to tenderness, attention, or proof of love?

The future is still unknown. But man aims at not engaging himself only with the past, but also with the present. He plans for the future, thinks, about that which does not yet exist. He tries to bring the future under his control and to organise it. One's imagination represents how one would cope with the future. Future plans are not limited to one's own future. In a comprehensive sense, one also feels responsible for other people. Here one can speak of the sense of justice, which every individual has. The injustice by close fellow beings, parents, siblings, situation teachers in professional and moral institutions can immensely influence the sense of justice and its impact on trust and hope.

The confrontation of the youth with justice and injustice in the world is of great importance. The problems that occur during puberty are also not senseless considering this aspect. The unrest in the world gives rise to fear, aggression, mental unrest and the feeling of injustice on one hand. On the other hand it gives us the chance to check traditions that bonus down and make them more humane. This would also affect a later partnership that we may form in life.

Many people build many walls, but very few bridges. (Isaac Newton)

**Sometimes, one lands up paying a high price for something which one would have actually got free of cost.
(Albert Einstein)**

76

Recognising the special qualities of the partner –
Love needs caring

The Moral of the Bitter Melon

A master had a servant, who was very devoted to him. One fine day, he gave his servant a melon, which looked very ripe and expensive on slicing. The servant took one bite after another, with relish, till he had eaten all of it. The master was shocked upon not being offered the melon once, whereupon, he took the last piece and ate it, only to find that the melon was excessively bitter. "Why is it so bitter? Didn't you find it bitter?" he asked the servant. "Yes, my master," he answered. "It was bitter but I have enjoyed the joys of your care and warmth so much, that a bitter melon was not a problem.

A 36-year-old officer explained that the attractive and confident behaviour of his wife had initially impressed him a lot. But then he went on to say, "My wife is moody and a blabber mouth. She is also stubborn and an extrovert. I am quiet, balanced, an introvert and diplomatic. My wife benefits more from my calm and balanced nature than I from her garrulous nature. In fact, she sometimes pushes herself into the focus which makes me seem like a weakling."

Here the flaw is the regulation of the relationship on the basis of mutual compromise. When one wishes to compensate for one's supposed flaws through the abilities of the partner, the partner's strength seems overpowering and make one's weaknesses and inabilities more evident. Therefore very often over a period of time the relationship comes to, "I don't want to suffer due to your nature, we are entirely different from each other."

When one exposes a certain shortcoming of the partner, it may also mean that he does not perceive his partner's personality per se. Due to unequal distribution of energies, certain areas are stressed upon and the rest are pushed aside.

Special Questions:

Have I understood my spouse well?

Have I expressed myself in an understandable manner?

Why couldn't he/she understand me better?

How did it lead to a misunderstanding?

Is it too demanding, when I am asked to confess the misunderstanding?

When my partner takes efforts to understand me, will I be able to compromise?

Can this problem be solved?

Do I want to solve this problem?

Can my partner rise up to my expectations?

Does he want the problem solved?

Have I begun making efforts to solve the problem?

Do I see our situation fairly and openly?

Do I express myself honestly?

Am I ready to lend an ear to my partner?

Am I ready to give time to my partner or for myself or do I expect changes to occur by themselves?

Do I expect the other to change or am I also ready for a self-change?

Do I want to give my partner and myself a chance?

Do I remain loyal to my partner at all times, even during a major conflict?

We do not judge our partner and his behaviour objectively. This perception actually differs from person to person, depending on experiences, and the deep-rooted emotional reaction and expectation that one has from his/her partner. The consequence of this subjectivity in perceiving the partner are misunderstandings, which one being a part of the cause, very rarely accepts. Very often, only a vague emotion is experienced. An interchange of roles strengthens the mutual understanding and ability to comprehend. The technique is very easy. For a week, the man does all the shopping and the woman takes up the responsibility of inviting the guests. Also, in matters of sexual intercourse the partners take initiatives alternately. This method, rather than being formal, can be quite adventurous for the ones involved in it. By this, they try to explore new areas of interaction and forms of relationships.

One who loves flowers, should at least have a positive relationship with them. But only a positive relationship is not sufficient; the plant can still wilt. One who loves plants should also know which flowers he prefers. One who loves flowers should also know what the plants need. He should provide them with water, clean air and sunlight. But after all this too his flowers can wilt. One who loves flowers, needs experience and the advice of those who have gathered experience in this field. Their advice helps in avoiding mistakes in cultivation and aids in balancing out the hindrances in growth.

Husband: Do you know sweetheart, I will work hard and one day we shall be rich.
Wife: We are already rich dear, because we have each other. One day we shall probably have money.

Question: Did you break up with your girlfriend because she wore spectacles?
Answer: No, she broke up with me because she had spectacles.

Question: How are you?
Answer: Unfortunately, not fine. My wife wants a divorce.
Question: But why so?
Answer: She says that I am cruel and that I don't take care of her as a responsibility. But I was so kind to her. Every morning I use to get her coffee to her bed, but only she needed it for to paint.

Love lives on loving trivialities.
(Theodore Fontane)

One must love, when one wants to be loved.

One who digs a pit for another falls in it himself –
Why revenge tastes bitter

Reward Shared

An itinerant preacher of the ancient time came with an important message. In an alien city, he wanted to give it personally to the king. Even after the ministers of the kingdom insisted him to give it to them, he stood firm on his decision. And, after having a word with the Wazir secretly, he was sent to the king. The king seemed to be very happy with the message of the preacher and told him to ask for anything that he wished for. To the shock of everyone the preacher asked for a hundred thrashings. After he received the first 50 of them, he shouted, "Wait! The Wazir should receive the other 50, as I had promised him half of my reward."

The 52-year-old wife of a renowned academician was going through depression, due to the crisis in her marriage. During this time, she turned to kleptomania. This made the husband so restless, that he was ready to let her undergo psychiatric treatment.

It was concluded that the patient was suffering due to lack of attention from her husband. He concentrated only on his work and she felt like a person undeserving of attention.

The kleptomania was a way out for her, to gain a little bit of attention from her husband all the while punishing him for the punishments that she had to undergo. But for this, she had to go through a lot of humiliation herself. Her revenge was unknowingly also directed towards herself.

Punishment can be practised in different forms and grades in a relationship by self-destruction or by harming others; "masochistic" or "sadistic". It can be practised in different areas.

Physical: Through denial of tenderness or through mishandling, so that the person has to consciously or unconsciously look for support. An example could be the denial of sex, used as a weapon.

Relationships: Through curbing or denial of social relations or exactly opposite to this, looking to some other rewarding relationship.

Imagination and Sensitivity: Through suffocating routines, which do not allow further progress. Through ignorance or disregard of the convictions of others.

In this context of "punishments in relationships", the basics of childhood play a very determining role. Basics, that become very transparent, when we observe. Discussed above are four areas of restricting love. Here we ask:

How did my parents treat my siblings and me?

How did my parents treat each other?

How were the relations of my parents with the rest of the world and at work?

How did my parents behave in regard to religion and the conception of world?

The forms of punishment used and the 'revenge' have their own history and reasons that are not formed only due to the concepts of sadism and masochism. We see the punishment for an autocratic act like some legal or parental punishment. Many times it happens in regard with the punishment that it becomes difficult to differentiate between the one who is punishing and the one who is being punished. The desire of sharing the pain and joy together is also maintained in the atmosphere of hatred during separation. The person who initially wanted to share the good, now wants to share the bad too, even when he himself has to suffer for it.

As explained a 48-year-old mother of four children said at the divorce, "I will make his life hell, so that he will never be happy with any other woman either."

Moral: The actual ability of "Justice" is the ability to consider the interest carefully in regard to self and others. One judges behaviour as unjust, when it is dictated on the basis of personal dislike or affection or bias, and not on the basis of practical thinking. The social aspect of this ability is to do social justice. Every person has a sense of justice. If his desire for justice is so much that he is prepared to hurt either himself or another then it is expressed immediately through retaliation and passive aggression.

Special Questions:

Who amongst you gives more importance to justice? (Justice and injustice in which situations and against whom?)

How do you react, when you are treated unjustly (professionally, in the family arena, etc.)?

Do you treat your partner justly (the children, the in-laws, the mediators, someone)?

Do you have or if you have problems of unjust behaviour (will you spare someone)?

83

Who did your parents hold for being just amongst you and your siblings (situations)?

Justice without love sees only performance and does only comparisons. Love without justice loses control over reality. Learn to balance love and justice. Do not believe your judgment, as soon as you discover the shadow of a personal motive behind it.
(Marie Von Ebener Eschenbach)

When we accept people the way they are, we spoil them; When we treat them as they should have been or should be, we take them there, where they should be.
(Johann Wolfgang Von Goethe)

Money is like a metal that conducts and also insulates well– Money as a substitute

True Frugality

A man accused of bribery was brought in front of the judge. As all the evidence was against him, the judgement appeared simple. The judge was a clever man. He offered the accused three choices, of which he had to undergo one as his punishment. The accused had to either pay 100 Tuman, or undergo 50 thrashings or he had to eat 5 kgs of onions.

'Eating 5 kgs of onions that should not be difficult', thought the convict, and bit the first onion. After he had eaten three fourths of a pound of raw onions, he was shaken by the horror of the sight of those notorious fruits of the field. He couldn't believe his eyes, and tears streamed down his face. "Your Majesty" he cried, "spare me from the onions. I would rather take the thrashing". He thought that in this way he would save his money, as he was a miser. The court usher undressed him, and laid him on the bench. The sight of the court usher and the hard cane shook the convict. With every thrashing on the back, he cried loudly and at the tenth, he wailed, "Great Ghazi, have mercy on me, spare me from the thrashings." The judge nodded. The accused had to undergo all the three punishments.

A 46-year-old woman married to a businessman, was well versed in her profession. She was of the opinion that marriages in which the basis of the relationship was a union of interests, were successful. The basic interest of both the partners being business and financial independence, the emotional aspect is given less importance.

After the sudden death of her husband, she was left with the task of managing the finances, which she had earlier enjoyed. Thereafter she felt distrust for all men; she imagined that all of them had an eye on her money. She refused to have deep social contacts and partnerships and discovered insecurities and depressive disagreement conditions and suicidal intentions. With the help of psychotherapy, the patient could relate to money and frugality or misery in a different way. She learnt to deal with money and not allow money to govern her life.

Activeness and performance is required for normalcy. How can one anyway speak of being active? Less is thought about activeness than about any other ability.

The wife of a workaholic husband doesn't suffer due to his activeness, but due to his failure in managing his time, patience and relations with her.

Performance orientation becomes a standard to which every individual becomes a subject. Many norms of performance are carried from the field of work to the field of family, in regard to the secondary qualities of orderliness, cleanliness, punctuality, and politeness. All these secondary qualities are learnt. The secondary qualities are connected with the important ones, but the right measures are constantly measured through life.

Special Questions:

Is the materialistic side, primary or secondary in the relationship?

What does financial security, financial success or loss mean to me?

What would I have done, if I didn't have any financial problems. Would I still be with my partner?

Am I able to manage business matters alone, without my partner, or am I dependent on him?

What would happen, if all of a sudden I/my partner had to live only on a bare minimum?

How have I learnt to deal with my money, finances and property?

For what do I use my property? For the people in whom I trust? For social development? (Here the question deals with one's responsibility of payment of taxes). For the needy in my country and in developing countries (in context to charity)?

Have I thought about what should be done with my property after me?

Even when one tries to dematerialise the relationship and love ideally, it is seen that the materialistic basis is stronger than the intensity of love. Therefore a business relationship does not seem to be different from this relationship. Lastly it becomes clearer by the flexibility of the relationship that divorce, which is of the more of practical sense, is a possibility. Money matters already play a role in the selection of a partner, even when the society is conservative and traditional. Birds of a feather flock together. One who hasn't acquired; remains a poor fellow, until he dies.

Moral:

It is sometimes necessary to consider one's own behaviour, to compare it with others and other cultures:

What do I possess which is a part of my entity and of which I can neither renounce, nor do I want to renounce and what is the problem due to it, which hinders me and my partners relationship?

From what have we acquired our possessions during the course of our development? What does possessing mean to me, to my partner, to other people, and to my conscience and how can I find new solutions and compromises?

A lady asked her best friend about her previous admirer, a rich old man, and received an answer, "I believe, he is fine. We had a business exchange with each other. Initially I had the experience and he the money, and now I have the money and he the experience".

Standard of living: One spends, that which one does not have, on the things, that one does not need, to impress people one does not like.

What do you have that makes you what you are?
Achievement and self-esteem

One more long programme

A businessman had 150 camels that carried his bags, and 40 slaves and servants who obeyed him. On certain evening he invited his friend, Saadi. The whole night he felt restless and spoke about the worries and needs of his profession. He told of his wealth in Turkey and goods in India, showed the documents of his lands and jewels. "Oh Saadi!", sighed the businessman. "Now I have to go on a journey. After this journey I will settle down with my earned peace, which I crave like no one in the world. I want to bring the Persian sulphur to China, as I have heard that it is good there. From there I want to take Chinese vases to Rome. Then my ship will take the Roman goods to India from where I want to take the Indian steel to Halab. From there I want to carry mirror and glass goods and from there I want to import velvet to Persia". With a dreamy expression, he told the reluctantly listening Saadi. "And then my life belongs to peace, consciousness and meditation, the highest aim of my life". (Saadi, Persian poet).

The report of a 38-year-old branch manager of a bank, who complained inner restlessness, depressing feelings, nervous breakdown, giddiness and other psychosomatic symptoms:

"The morning begins with me giving my letters for distribution, but I keep on rechecking to make sure that it is

89

done in proper order. Then come numerous reports that have to be forwarded immediately. And according to the type of report, the acceptance time of exchange varies between 11 a.m. and 1 p.m.

At 11: 10 my wife calls up, and I don't have time for her, which makes me feel sorry. I want to go to the toilet and there comes the next customer. Even when I don't have time for him, at 11:30 starts the exchange.

I try and make my conversations as short as possible. I notice how the reports are laid on the table for correction. I cannot even go through the reports, as I have to talk to my customers. I know the case of a colleague from Stuttgart, whose faulty report was forwarded, which cost the bank 45,000 DM.

Lastly, it is time for numerous phone calls at 1 o'clock. I go with some of my colleagues to eat lunch. And by God's grace, there is seldom any problem there. After my lunch, I call up some more customers and explain some offers. Besides that, I think over certain suggestions for current customer management. The head inquires early in the next day, about the work done. The statement to the personnel manager is still to be given. I have to somehow adjust it in my schedule.

At 4:30 p.m. I am done with 78 telephone calls and 13 customers. At home I can very well rest, but I think very often for five minutes in peace about the major tasks that I have to carry out next day."

People's efforts finally bring them success due to luck and self-effort. But the way towards this is mostly down a narrow path. Calming the restless soul will bring about positive and creative thought. It is ability which is new to Westerners, but which can be learnt.

When the balance in life is upset, then the individual reacts with physical and psychic disorders. Therefore one asks the following questions:

How is my relationship with myself? Do I spare time for my physical needs like sleep, nutrition, aesthetics, sports, sex, physical contact, tenderness, and health?

How do I relate to my profession? Have I chosen my profession willingly or have I been forced into it?

Did I have nothing other than this profession to pursue?

Do I like the work that I am given?

Do I work only to earn money and to afford certain things, or does the profession satisfy my intellect, or has it become my need?

Do I have conflicts in my profession?

Am I promoted or demoted? Do I like my profession, but not my colleagues?

How far can I contribute in the area of social development? How far do I observe ethics and morals in my profession?

What is my relationship with my partners and my social surroundings?

Do I have a good relationship with my wife/husband and my children?

Do I spare time for my family? Do I confide in my family?

Do I have consideration for my family?

Do I only follow obedience and politeness and give importance to exchange of thoughts?

How is my relationship with my relatives, friends and colleagues?

How is my relationship with my countrymen and the other people?

Am I social?

Do I have prejudices, fears and aggression against certain individuals or groups?

How do I view my future? Am I satisfied with my present?

Do I foresee possibilities of progress or possibilities of stagnation?

What are my aims and what are the causes of my orientation system?

What does life mean to me? How do I deal with the difficulties that arise in the other fields?

Am I ready to express my opinion frankly, even when I see myself losing friendly support?

What part does music, art, painting, and literature play in my life?

How do I imagine my life after death?

A man is proud of his devotion to duty. But soon, gets unhappy and becomes lazy towards them. (Eugen Roth)

Woodcutting is loved, as one finds success very soon.
(Albert Einstein)

It is not sufficient to know but one should make use of knowledge. It is not sufficient to wish, one should turn wishes to reality.
(Johann Wolfgang von Goethe)

One should think well about what one wants.
One may get it.

One who wants to achieve,
should remain cheerful.

Success is an end result. It should
never be seen as the aim.
(Gustave Flaubert)

Many ruin their health in the first half
of their life to earn money and success,
and spend the money in the second
half to regain health.

Don't be misled by the first impression–
See the reality of others

The Lantern as Protection

On a dark night, a blind man was going with a lantern in one hand a jug full of olives on his shoulders, through the narrow lanes of the bazaars. There he met a friend, who said to him, "My friend, day and night are the same for you. What is the use of this lantern for you? The blind man smiled and answered, "The lantern is not for me, but for you, so that you will be careful and won't dash against the jug on my shoulder."

A young man talks about the difficulties in perceiving himself and others with respect to their special characteristics: At the age of 18 or 19, I came to the university clinic for youth psychiatry for four weeks, because I was suffering from a major inferiority complex. I used to wish to hide in a mouse hole, was unable to laugh, was tilled with embarrassment, used to stammer, used to find myself ugly... For two whole weeks I was staring at a nurse. After reading my medical reports, she would come to my room every night. She slept with me. She was my first wife and was older than me. She said to me, "I love my fiance and I am fond of you." I could not understand this. I wanted to marry her as I would have married any girl who showed an interest in me.

Every relationship requires a great effort to involve oneself with the thoughts and ideas, the interests and characteristics

94

of the partner. One can make these efforts only if the partner does not require your help in any of these areas. This was an experiment of the blind leading the blind. Such people tend to choose partners that do not possess characteristics of a confident person. Both of us were equal; no one could dictate terms. My wife was also no genius.

According to the mechanism of the two blind-type a partnership is possible due to the closeness between the partners. Each partner seems to exude thoughts that say, I need you to prove to me that you are inferior to me and I am superior to you. This attitude offers a sense of security, which is similar to that of the poorest, most uneducated white person, who lives in the American slums and feels superior to coloured people and Puerto Ricans. As much as he may hate them because he feels threatened by them, he also needs them in his imaginary world to improve his social position.

This form of relationship is mostly symmetrical i.e., both the partners equally participate in it. Man needs others to give him the needed reaction. Actually in this case it is not important to know which qualities the partner possesses, because it is not needed. What the partner offers, irritates. His incapacities are taken into consideration, whereas his positive characteristics are ignored. So for example, the unreliability of a person will be taken into consideration. In the case of a woman, everything is ignored on a large scale what she does in the household, for the children and for the partner, keeping firmly in mind that she is not employed or is not so successful in her profession as compared to her husband.

In order not to have a double-blind type partnership, it is necessary to recognise the specific individual strength and capacity of the partner. This does not mean that he should compete with others of his age and generation with respect to his abilities and prove himself as the best. It appears to be more important to recognise the special abilities and to support their development. Many people are practical; others possess more abstract abilities. Many show organisation abilities; others appear to be successful in the artistic field.

We cannot ignore our own incapability and that of others. Realisation of incapabilities offers the possibility to correct them. The uniqueness of a person depends on his personal activities and his individual efforts. He is not only the product of body and environment, but develops himself continuously. The uniqueness of a person helps in moulding his actual capacities. Every activity can be categorised as active and passive.

Special Questions

To be active means: to be punctual/unpunctual, to be tidy/untidy, to be honest/dishonest. What does it mean to me?

To be passive means: How do I react to the punctuality demands or unpunctuality of others? How do I get along with the disorder or cleanliness of my partner? Can I bear the demands of justice or injustice of my partner?

The position of a partner depends not only upon the actual capabilities, which he expresses, but also whether he demands active behaviour or expects passive behaviour. Often the realisation of this double-mindedness is the decisive factor in solving conflicts. One is not always treated justly, and sometimes if necessary, one should accept injustice without breaking the relationship.

"If I am the first one whom you kissed," she said, "how could you do it so well?"

96

He answered, "And if I am the first one whom you are kissing, then how do you know that I am doing it well?

It is the fate of a person: When a couple fights, they get to know each other better. (Leopold von Ranke)

One realises the value of humans and diamonds, only after one observes them carefully. The Oriental wisdom of life.

Positive psychotherapy: The holistic model with education, self-help and psychotherapeutic methods

The positive procedure can be compared with the following situation:

A man realised that he was in debt. He was not able to sleep because of these thoughts. He was suffering from depression and wanted to end his life. He told his good friend about this. The friend listened to all his worries very patiently. But later, he spoke nothing about the debts. Instead the friend spoke about what the man possessed about his money, and his friends, who were ready to help him. This surprised the man, but suddenly his view towards the situation changed. He felt that he need not worry about the debts, and realised that he had enough power and numerous ways to solve the problem.

Positive psychotherapy has a multistage treatment plan. Positive psychotherapy is not limited to the immediate therapeutic situation, but rather reaches beyond this, to the patient's extra-therapeutic social relations. The patient does not just assumes the role of a patient, but becomes the therapist of his immediate reference groups and especially of his conflict partner. This double role of the patient, as a patient and a therapist at the same time is an essential characteristic of positive psychotherapy.

When you need a helping hand, look for it at the end of your own arm.

The Development of Positive Psychotherapy Under the Transcultural Aspect

An important motivation for me was that I myself was in a transcultural situation (Germany-Iran). In that situation, I was aware that, conduct, habits and attitudes were judged differently in different cultural groups.

Concept	West	East
Illness	When someone is ill, he loves to be left in peace. Very few people visit him. Visits are considered social control.	When someone is ill, his bed is shifted to the living room. E.g. in the case when a leg is fractured. The patient is at the centre of activity and is visited by a number of family members, relatives and friends. Absence of a visitor would be considered as an offence and lack of sympathy.
Death	"We request not to have a condolence visit." "I must deal with my fate alone." "Now I must bear the sorrow all alone."	The members of the family, are visited for 8-40 days by their relatives, friends and other fellow beings, who give them a feeling of security. "Sorrow becomes less when it is shared."

An experience, which I had as a child, in Teheran dealt with prejudices, mostly of a religious kind. As a member of the Bahai faith, we had conflicts between Islamic, Christian and Jewish schoolmates and teachers. This forced me to think about the relationship between religions and the relationship of people with eachother.

I have seen the families of my schoolmates, and tried to understand their conduct based on the ideology of their faiths. Later, I witnessed a similar confrontation during my specialist training. I noticed how tense the relationship of a psychiatrist, neurologist, internist and psychotherapist was, and how the different views collided violently with each other.

I engaged myself with the contents and backgrounds of such tensions. This experience was important for me, as I understood other forms and organisations of the family unit. The family in which I grew up, included not only my parents, brothers and sisters, but a large number of relatives and other family members to whom we were bound as a family. Here I experienced the feeling of group belongingness, and mutual care and security, but there was also a feeling of dependence and restriction. The typical European family that is worried about the independence of the individual appears to be a supplement of the oriental system with all the advantages and disadvantages. According to me, family as an institution proves to be one of the important coordinating points, which shows how abilities and possibilities of a person can be developed or suppressed. In this way, the family puts restrictions and influences the choice of partner, the choice of profession, relationships with other people and the person's future.

These experiences and thoughts of mine lead to the conclusion that even in psychotherapy, humans are not considered isolated individuals but relations with fellow beings and transcultural situations are taken into consideration.

The transcultural approach is like a red thread in the total positive family therapy. Therefore we take this approach separately into consideration, because the transcultural aspect also offers material to understand the individual conflicts. Above all, this aspect possesses an extraordinary social meaning which we see reflected in problems of immigrants, development aids, difficulties which arises in the environment with members of other cultural systems, problems of transcultural partnerships, prejudices and the abilities to overcome them, alternative models, which originate from other cultures. In this context political topics can also be mentioned, which result from the transcultural situations.

Positive psychotherapy and family therapy represent a form of short-term psychotherapy as the transcultural and interdisciplinary aspect which is related to the deep psychological procedure.

1. The Positive Human Picture: The Positive Approach

Basic questions:
1. What do all people have in common?
2. How are they differentiated?

For instance, just as a seed possesses a multitude of capacities which are unfolded through the influence of the environment, for example, the earth, rain, the gardener, etc. In such a way, a human being also develops his capacities in close relation with his environment. Underlying the concept of positive psychotherapy and family therapy is the conception that every person has two basic capacities, i.e., the capacity to know and capacity to love (emotionality). According to the condition of the body, the environment and the time in which a person lives, certain basic capacities are developed and lead to an unmistakable structure of characteristics (Peseschkian, 1991).

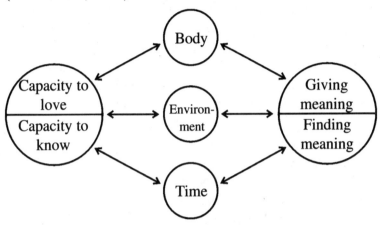

Basic capacities and development conditions for giving meaning (religion) and finding meaning.

Capacity to love means: The ability to love and to be loved. This leads to further development in the primary capacities such as ability to love, to be patient, to make time for oneself, to develop contacts, to give and take affection and sexuality, the ability to trust, to have hope, to believe, the ability to doubt, to manage certainties and to establish unity.

Capacity to know: The ability to learn and to teach. Through this capacity, secondary abilities are developed, such as punctuality, cleanliness, tidiness, obedience, politeness, honesty/frankness, trust, justice, hard work/performance, saving, reliability/accuracy, conscience.

The primary and the secondary capacities can be called 'actual capacities'. In day-to-day description and evaluation and in judging partners, the secondary capacity plays an important role. One who finds a partner kind and nice, justifies his views with: 'He is decent and respectable and hence one can rely on him.' On the other hand, one says: 'I don't like him, because he is messy, unpunctual, unfair, impolite, cunning, and very lazy.' Similarly, the consequences of corresponding mental and physical experiences are common. For example, pedantry, disorder, ritualised cleanliness, untidiness, exaggerated punctuality, unpunctuality, unreliability, besides social conflict, psychological and psychosomatic qualities such as anger, aggression and imitation lead to consequences in the psychological field, in the respiratory system, in the gastro-enteric area, intestinal area, movement of the body, in the nervous system, in the genital area and the skin.

"When I hear that in school an arithmetic problem is given, I feel restless till my daughter Renate (nine-year-old) comes with a solution. When the work is done, my restlessness disappears. When there is a bad outcome, I feel a stabbing pain in my chest." (32-years-old, mother of three children having a heart problem and disturbed circulation system)

"My husband always says, 'We must save electricity, a 40 watt bulb is sufficient, instead of a 60 watt bulb.' He has adopted this idea from his mother, who was sometimes very mean. On the other hand, he showers his children with toys." (33-year-old wife, sexually deprived)

"I have heart and stomach problems, since I have known that my husband is not loyal to me. For many years he managed to hide it. Even in other matters, he was not open. The children also suffered due to our tension". (45-year-old housewife)

"If I have not cleaned the room, it means that I don't love you anymore". This frightened me. Today I am more pedantic and I often get into conflicts with my husband and children." (39-year-old wife, chronic constipation and insomnia)

"One who tells lies once; one does not believe him even if he speaks the truth". Because my mother always blamed me with lies, I finally decided that I could lie coolly since nobody believed me" (Officer, 34-years-old, problems in professional life.)

There is a tendency in the West to overlook the primary capacities for example, social contact and to lay emphasis on the secondary ones, for instance the ability to perform. Against this, the East tends to emphasise the primary capabilities, while neglecting the secondary ones.

2. The Types of Procedure: *Conflict Dynamic and Content of Conflict—Four Qualities of Life Correspond to the Four forms of Dealing with Conflict.*

Despite all cultural and social differences and uniqueness of every person, observe that all use the typical way in dealing with conflicts, while coping with their problems. When we have a problem we feel angry, burdened and misunderstood. We are under continuous strain and see life as meaningless. The problem can be solved with the help of the four forms of dealing with conflicts, which are classified into four media of ability to know.

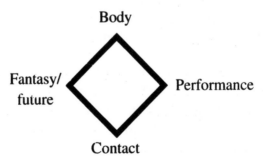

Four Qualities of Life
Four Forms of Dealing with Conflicts.
(Four Media of Perception)

105

1. Body (Medium of Sensory)
2. Performance (Medium of Mind Perception)
3. Contact (Medium of Tradition)
4. Fantasy (Medium of Intuition)

Every person facing a problem uses these four forms of dealing with conflicts. According to positive psychotherapy, people who do not have conflicts, are not healthy, but those who have learned to tackle them, are healthy. This means that these four areas of life (Body, Performance, Contact (social), Fantasy) should not be neglected, but the energy of an individual (not necessary his time) should be divided equally in the four areas. The four areas correspond to a rider, who motivates (performance) to move towards the aim (fantasy). For this, he needs a good and well-groomed horse (body) and in case the horse throws him off, he needs a helper, who will revive him (contact).

According to my observation in Europe and North America, the areas of body and performance are important forms of dealing with conflicts, while the Oriental tendency is towards '(social) contact' and 'fantasy'. In spite of this tendency, individuals develop their unique forms of reaction, and establishes uniqueness of the personality.

If an imbalance occurs in the four qualities of life, it results in four forms of escape. Man escapes from illnesses (somatic forms of disturbance), from activity and performance (rationalisation, as in problems of performance and adjustment) or from society (idealisation or reduction, as in effective disturbances and changes of social behaviour) from fantasy (disownment due to worries, phobias, panic attacks, and illusive disturbances).

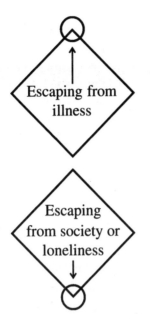

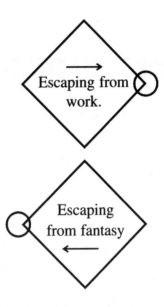

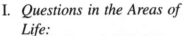

I. *Questions in the Areas of Life:*

Body

1. What health complaints do you have, which organs are more affected?

2. Is it important for you that your partner should be good-looking?

3. Which organ of your body is affected by your anger?

4. What influence does your illness have on your feeling and on your future?

II. *Questions in the Areas of Life:*

Performance

1. Which activities would you like to practise performance? Are you satisfied with your profession?

2. When you judge a person, how important is his intelligence and social prestige for you?

3. With what do you engage yourself more: your profession or your family?

4. Between your parents, who lays more emphasis on performance?

III. Questions in the Areas of Life

(Social) Contact

1. Who is the most sociable in your family?
2. What would you do to avoid guests: saying that you have very little time, that they cost money, or that they are untidy?
3. How do you feel when you are in the company of many people?
4. Do you stick to your familiar (religious, political) traditional festivals?
5. In your childhood did you have many friends or were you isolated?

IV. Questions in the Areas of Life

Fantasy/Future

1. Do you think you are an optimist or a pessimist?
2. Do you think of your past? Do you engage yourself with your future?
3. If you wish to exchange your roles with someone, with whom would you like to do so? Why?
4. According to you, what influence do religious and ideological concepts have on the upbringing of children, choice of a partner and your relationship with fellow beings?
5. What is your reaction on the members of other religious sects and representatives of other ideological convictions?

3. Five steps of Positive Psychotherapy

With positive psychotherapy, a stressed person mobilises his self-helping ability in a relatively short time. An improvement takes place after six to ten therapy sessions. The five steps are always dynamically connected.

Step (i): Observation/Distancing

Every person who takes part in a conflict, behaves at first as someone who stands so near a picture, that he can touch it with his nose. He sees only a small part without experiencing the whole. The first step includes acknowledging the stress factors and comprehending conflicts and describing its contents. The patient writes as much as possible regarding what or whom he gets annoyed with, and which occasions he finds pleasant. At this stage, the process of learning to discriminate begins. One starts to understand the conflict and to describe it in terms of contents.

What can you do by yourself?

Write down what you feel annoyed with and pleasant with. Describe these situations.

Do not criticise, but confine yourself to the description.

Do not speak with a third person about your problems, but notice carefully, under what circumstances the problems arise and when they do not.

Develop alternatives: How will you behave in a specific conflict?

Step (ii): Making an Inventory

Making an inventory is about the art of coping with conflicts and stress. With the help of questions, the four areas dealing with conflicts are discussed. The intention behind this is to get to the root of the conflicts and to learn how to deal with them.

What can you do by yourself?

Write down the areas in which you have problems. Are they related to body/sense, performance, contact or fantasy?

Go back to the past and think about how the relationship with your parents and other family members was. Who was your idol?"

What was your family's motto?

What do you think is more emphasised, when you go through these questions? Do your ideas differ with that of your partner's thus leading to misunderstandings and conflicts?

Step (iii): Situational Encouragement

We engage ourselves with the things we find positive and stimulating, and also do the negative and unpleasant things bravely. This step therefore keeps us away from conflicts and question for example what holds the family or partnership together firmly, in spite of the conflicts? Even stories, parables, and maxims can ease the change of position and can help to get away from the persistent series of old problems.

What can you do by yourself?

What is positive and negative depends on the respective concepts, which are used as fixed rules:

Ask your fellowmen, what expectations and attitudes are responsible for their behaviour that creates problems for them.

In the first and second week try not to criticise others, but try to encourage them, so that the positive capacities can be strongly praised.

Even paradoxical encouragement is possible. Encouraging others in their problematic areas can help them to develop another perspective.

Introduce your concepts and opposite concepts in the form of stories and maxims. e.g., "We don't suit each other" "There are many contradictions."

Step (iv): Verbalisation

To overcome speechlessness and language distortion, step-by-step communication is practised with the partner. As the capacities of understanding are promoted in the earlier steps, a direct argument begins to solve the conflicts instead of ending it.

What can you do by yourself?

Talk with your partner, family, colleagues or in a self-help group about your problem.

Try to know the opinion and position of others and put yours against it.

Search for a solution that is useful for all. This is possible only when you express it honestly.

The temporary exchange of functions and roles can promote understanding for each other.

Step (v): Broadening of Goals

The neurotic narrowing of the field of vision is purposefully demolished. One learns not to carry the conflicts over into other domains of behaviour, rather to steer them towards new and inexperienced aims. The broadening of goals helps the person to make plans for the future, enhance the four qualities of life and the actual capacities, and to develop new behaviour and contacts.

What can you do by yourself?

What aims and wishes do you have for your future?

What will you do when you have no problems?
Extend your aims to the areas of actual capacities and develop new possibilities to deal with the conflicts.

Help for Changing Position

Stories, parables, proverbs, and maxims are a way to mobilise the resources of people instead of engaging oneself with old problems. They make the mental and emotional exchange of position easy. But even within the framework of therapist-patient-relationship, they offer the person involved important initiatives. The stories are not used randomly in positive psychotherapy, but are used purposefully in the five-step therapy.

**A person is considered a mine,
enriched with precious gems.
(From the Bahai scripts)**

**Intelligence without love is cold,
Love without intelligence is naive,
Intelligence with love is Wisdom.**

112

The importance of stories, maxims and humour in daily life

Life Hangs Often by a Thread

After his death, an isolated and aggressive man met the angel of death. The angel said to him, "Have you done any good deed in your life? If yes, this good deed can help you get an entry in to paradise." The man answered, "I cannot remember any good deed that I did in my life." The angel said, "Think hard, you will perhaps remember something." The man then remembered one such deed. He remembered that once, while taking a walk in the woods, he had given way to a spider, instead of crushing it under his feet. The angel smiled, and a thread of a spider's web came down from heaven on which the man was supposed to climb to paradise. But out of fear that the thread would break, he blew it away. At that very moment, the thread actually broke, and the man fell down to the hell. He heard the voice of the angel of death, "Unfortunately your egoism and self-centeredness have transformed the only good deed that you had done, into a curse." (This story is depicted and interpreted in various forms in different cultures. In the Brazilian culture it was adapted by Paolo Coelho.)

The fundamental feature of working with such stories is to try to address not only the logic of the reader, but also his inherent capability to fantasies. For this reason, the isolated train of thoughts is illustrated through psalms, picture stories, stories, and aphorisms. They make available not only information sources, but also an oasis for relaxation.

Oriental and Occidental mythology and psalms have common roots and have often been used to illustrate history.

Functions of Stories and Parables

It is said that the function of stories is to ignite the process of thinking profoundly about interpersonal relationships. They also serve to increase knowledge and spiritual progress attained by the confrontation in stories.

Mirror Function

The picturesque depictions allow the reader to associate himself with the story. The listener can align his needs with the story and deduce morals according to his own psychic makeup.

Model Function

Stories are models. They introduce conflict situations and give suggestions for possible solutions and their consequences.

Mediator Function

In a psychotherapeutic situation, the therapist and the patient's confrontations are exposed in the story. Nothing about the patient is discussed. Thus a three-dimensional process comes into action: patient-story-therapist.

Depot Effect

Because of its vivid descriptions, the stories and parables are good to maintain and can be easily used in other situations. They are applicable not only in the prevailing treatment but also in the day-to-day life of the patient. The stories thus have a depot effect i.e., they have an after affect and make the patient independent of the therapist.

Stories and Parables as Carriers of Tradition

When we turn ourselves to the content of the stories and the embodied concepts, we find behaviour and attitudes that support one's own tradition's behaviour and conflict.

Stories and Parables as Transcultural Mediator

Stories of other cultures bring information about the rules and concepts that are important in the other culture. It shows other ways of thinking and enables us to widen our own repertoire of concepts, values and conflict solutions.

Stories and Parables as Help for Regression

Stories open up the door to fantasy, imaginative thinking, marvel, and wonder. Stories and parables are to some extent the carriers of creativity and thus a medium between desires and reality. The stories thus mould us in accordance with personal wishes and aims of the near and far future. Stories give space for utopic dreams the alternative for reality.

Stories as Antithetical Concepts

Through the story, the therapist does not allude to asserted theory, but offers an antithetical concept to the patient, which the patient can accept or reject. Through the stories, ambiguous information can be given consciously, through a familiar system or through a totally different social system, which can be grasped partially in a conflict situation.

Stories are thereby merely a special form of human communication, through which even concepts are exchanged.

Change of Location

Most of the stories and parables go beyond the pure description and have surprise endings, known as optical illusions. Without giving much trouble to the teller or the listener, a change of location is accomplished, which is perceived as a surprise, and an 'Aha' experience is achieved.

Practice of Humour in Profession and Partnership

Patient: Doctor, my husband speaks uninterruptedly in sleep. What should I do?
Doctor: Dear lady, it would be best if you let him speak in the day.

Boss to the employee: You sleep for half an hour during working hours.
Employee: Yes Mr. Director, but the whole day I dreamt only of my work.

A patient bitterly opposed to his operation. "I would prefer death to letting myself be operated upon." At that the chief doctor smilingly bent over his bed, and said "My dear, do not make such a fuss. At times, both are connected to each other."

O Doctor, I am scared! This is my first operation. The friendly young doctor replied, "mine as well."

"I'd like to see the boss."
"The boss is not available."
"But I just saw him through the window."
"Quite possible. But the boss had seen you first!

Question: Was it really love at first sight with Helga?
Answer: Yes, I always do it that way. It saves so much of time."
Wife: What would you do if I leave you?
Husband: "The same as what you would do."

Wife: "Ha, you scoundrel! I had always suspected it, but today you yourself revealed it."

A mother talking to her friend about bringing up children said, "My husband and I agree totally on certain issues. Whenever there is a quarrel, we send our children out to play." "O! That is why they have become so tanned!" said the friend.

Self-experience

We have got to know many things through stories, maxims, humour, fables, and fairy tales. We have learnt to love them, be indifferent to them or to deny them. Some of the questions can help us understand and clarify the reason of our attitude towards stories:

Who read out and narrated the stories to you (father, mother, siblings, grand-parents, aunt, nursery teacher etc.)?

Can you think of situations in which the stories were narrated? How did you feel?

What do you think of fairy tales? Which parable comes to your mind instantly?

Who is your favourite author?

Which maxims and concepts mean a lot to you?

Collect your bright days for the rainy days of your life

The Optimist Chess Loser

A chess player, who convinced about his capabilities, had a stroke of bad luck in one game. He lost three consecutive rounds. On the next day, one of his friends met him and asked, "How many rounds did you play yesterday?'

The chess player answered, "Three!" The friend asked, "How did the party go?"

The answer was, "You know, I lost the first one, my opponent did not lose the second round, and as far as the third round is concerned, he refused to declare the round undeclared."

A 38-year-old patient with self-respect problem and the fear of his future before and after treatment:

I can do what I want.
I am independent.

Although everything has not happened the way I had imagined, it was still quite good. (I faced many failed attempts) My family takes pride in me. They can rely on me, they do not need to worry about anything: I am indispensable.

If I am jobless, I can't take care of my family anymore. No job, no money, no house. Nobody believes me. I think, everybody thinks I will do something good. I lie; I cannot communicate, do not trust myself anymore when amongst people and in the market. Why am I living?

I'll die; my life has come to an end. What will my family do without me? What will my daughter be? She needs me. I can't take it anymore. I don't know what I have. I think that the doctor doesn't believe me. I'm told that I'm healthy. In spite of that I have problems. I don't have courage to go to the doctor, because I've been there many a time without an appointment.

Changed the doctor. I'm happy; I try to narrate my problems, I think, the doctor thinks, I work out, because I should be physically healthy. I don't know how to share my condition with the doctor. The doctor says that it's a disease. He told me that I really have health problems. I don't lie.

Thoughts after clinical treatment:
Hopefully the fear doesn't arise again. It's good that I have the feeling that I'm being believed. I can communicate again and restart mixing with people.

Goal
Optimism, positive thoughts, new missions in life, no fear of the future, to make every day a bright day. Every dark cloud has a silver lining!

119